CICERO
MURDER AT LARINUM

CICERO
MURDER AT LARINUM
from the *Pro Cluentio*

SELECTED AND EDITED BY
H. GROSE-HODGE

PUBLISHED BY BRISTOL CLASSICAL PRESS
GENERAL EDITOR: JOHN H. BETTS

(BY ARRANGEMENT WITH THE SYNDICATE OF THE CAMBRIDGE UNIVERSITY PRESS)

This impression 2002

First published in 1932 by Cambridge University Press

Reprinted (with permission) 1992 by
Bristol Classical Press
an imprint of
Gerald Duckworth & Co. Ltd.
61 Frith Street, London W1D 3JL
Tel: 020 7434 4242
Fax: 020 7434 4420
inquiries@duckworth-publishers.co.uk
www.ducknet.co.uk

A catalogue record for this book is available
from the British Library

ISBN 0 86292 093 0

Printed in Great Britain by
Antony Rowe Ltd, Eastbourne

Cover illustration: Cicero from a portrait bust, Vatican Museums, Rome.
[Drawing by Jean Bees]

CONTENTS

PREFACE

This volume contains a Latin thriller. It is the narrative of "the most sensational *cause célèbre* bequeathed to us by antiquity". It is intended to appeal to the modern boy. Had the dignity of a University Press permitted, it might have been entitled

MORE AND BETTER MURDERS

OR

OPPIANICUS, THE MASTER CROOK OF LARINUM

It probably justifies better than most modern thrillers the proud boast that it contains a murder on every page.

But there is more in it than that. It contains, in addition to murders, one of the finest pieces of narrative prose in the Latin language, set forth in a style unsurpassedly lucid and pure. No harm will befall the morals of any boy who reads this shocking but absorbing record—it all happened too long ago—and nothing but good can result to his Latin prose composition.

So long ago is it since the characters in Latin literature lived, that the reflection of the average boy after reading about them is too often apt to be "can these bones live?" This volume supplies the corrective. Thanks to the genius of Cicero the characters in it are still alive—and very much alive —after 2000 years. They are real people; and the moving story of their love affairs and family feuds, their crimes and intrigues, will help to remind a youthful reader that Latin was not always a dead language.

This volume claims, then, to "combine instruction with amusement", and offers something more palatable, perhaps, than Livy or Ovid can provide, to the boy who has grappled with Caesar and is not yet of an age to appreciate Vergil. As an introduction to Cicero, too, it is surely more suited to a lad in his teens than the *de Senectute* and more worthy of the orator than the (apparently) inevitable *de Imperio.*

The text is that of Prof. Ramsay, mostly as emended by Sir William Peterson and Mr Fausset, to whose exhaustive editions I have been indebted throughout the preparation of this volume.

I gratefully acknowledge the help of my colleague, Mr E. W. Davies, in the preparation of the Notes.

H. G-H.

Bedford
May 1931

INTRODUCTION

The narrative portions of the *pro Cluentio* which compose this volume are interesting without being difficult. Anyone who supposes that Cicero's style was always rhetorical and involved will realize his mistake when he has read this story, of which the language is so plain and simple as almost to conceal its perfect art. It is, indeed, spoken Latin in its purest and most direct form.

The difficulty—such as it is—lies not in the Latin in which the speech was composed, but in the complexity of the case which the orator was pleading—a case described by J. A. Froude as "a drama of real life played out in the last days of the Republic"; for in it so many actors have their rôles and so intricate is the plot that we are apt to become confused unless we make ourselves acquainted with the characters and their story beforehand, as was the audience to whom the speech was originally addressed.

The setting of the story is for the most part the *municipium* or county town of Larinum, not far from the Gulf of Venice, and the period within which it falls is one of the most troublous in the history of Rome, when the decline of the Republic had set in and its fall might be delayed but could not be prevented. The senatorial oligarchy was in the last phase of its long struggle with democracy, a struggle which left both Senate and People at the mercy of the Caesars.

The early years of the last century B.C. saw fought to a conclusion another issue of long standing, that between the citizens of Rome and their *socii*, the inhabitants of Italy, to whom they still obstinately denied the privileges of citizenship. This "Social" war broke out in 91 B.C. It was over by 88 B.C., and the Italians were Roman citizens at last, but it brought into rivalry two men, Marius and Sulla, who were to carry on in the years that followed a yet more deadly civil war in the names of the People and the Senate. First Marius, then Sulla, gained the upper hand; then Sulla went to fight against a foreign enemy in Asia and Marius recaptured Rome, and held it till Sulla returned and drove him out again. Not only the battles between them had cost the country dear in lives and property: more of both were sacrificed by the cruel proscriptions—the wholesale executions of the defeated party and confiscation of their goods—which marked the temporary triumph of either cause.

Our story deals with private rather than with public feuds: most of the events which it records took place between 82 and 72 B.C., the decade following the death of Marius. But the actors in it had grown up accustomed to tales, and even sights, of bloodshed and consequently disposed to think lightly of the sanctity of human life. The crimes committed at Larinum were in some cases the direct outcome of the civil wars, and in all cases may have been made more possible by the kind of post-war mentality which in our own time has caused so marked an increase in crimes of violence.

Larinum at this period seems to have contained three leading families, the Aurii, the Cluentii and the Oppianici, each of which, as is so often the case in similar society in England, had connexions by marriage with the other two. Their names and relationships will be found in the family trees set out below, and should be carefully studied.

The Aurii and the Cluentii were eminently respectable people, possessing not only wealth but a strong sense of responsibility and local patriotism. Not so the Oppianici, whose leading member, Statius Albius Oppianicus, is the villain of the piece. His evil life had already brought him into disrepute: he was, indeed, suspected of having poisoned his first wife, Cluentia (aunt of Cicero's client), and more than suspected of having murdered a young rake called Asuvius and having forged his will. The fact is that having squandered his own and his wife's fortunes he needed money; and to get money he was prepared to stick at nothing, as the rest of this story will show.

Oppianicus planned on a large scale and he aimed at nothing less than the acquisition of the entire fortunes of all three families. The first to be attacked were the Aurii, the chief representative of whom was an old lady called Dinaea, with her three sons and a daughter. Here is their family tree: those murdered by Oppianicus are marked †, those married to him *:

THE AURII

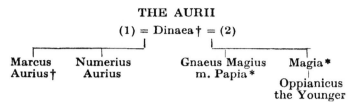

(1) = Dinaea † = (2)

Marcus Auriust, Numerius Aurius, Gnaeus Magius m. Papia*, Magia* Oppianicus the Younger

Related to the Aurii were Aulus Aurius †; Aulus Aurius Melinus † the husband of Cluentia, sister of Cicero's client, and probably the father of Lucius Aurius †; and Auria †, wife of Gaius Oppianicus, brother of the villain, Statius Albius Oppianicus.

One of Dinaea's sons, Marcus Aurius, had disappeared at the time of the Social War and had not been heard of since; and when the unexpected story of his survival in a distant slave prison reached Larinum, Oppianicus took prompt and effective measures to have him murdered by a hired assassin.

News travelled slowly in those days, and before his crime was known at Larinum Oppianicus set about reducing further the number of those who might divide the family property. Another of Dinaea's sons, Numerius Aurius, had died leaving his money to his half-brother, Gnaeus Magius. Then Gnaeus Magius died (no one quite knew how), leaving his money to be divided between his mother Dinaea and his nephew, Oppianicus the Younger. Thus Dinaea alone stood between the elder Oppianicus and the prize which would be his through his son's inheritance. He therefore poisoned her; and as she had left only part of her wealth to his son, her grandson, he got hold of her will and made the necessary alterations.

Meanwhile the news reached Larinum that Marcus Aurius, long lost and recently found again, had been murdered by Oppianicus' agent. At this the surviving relatives of Dinaea raised such an outcry that Oppianicus had to flee for his life to the camp of one of Sulla's generals. But he was a man who knew how to turn even his misfortunes to account; and he soon returned, armed with powers from the Dictator to proclaim martial law and to purge Larinum of all those who professed democratic sympathies. By the time he had carried out these orders not a male of the house of Aurius was left alive. So careful was he to leave no one who might give evidence against him, that he even included among his victims the wretch whom he had hired to murder Marcus Aurius.

To secure for himself the property of the Oppianici was a comparatively simple matter, as will be seen from their family tree:

THE OPPIANICI
```
                              |
        ┌─────────────────────┴──────────────────┐
  Statius Albius Oppianicus          Gaius Oppianicus†
m. 1 Cluentia† 2 Magia 3 Papia—a son†      m. Auria†
                   |    4 Novia—a son†
                   |    5 Sassia
                   |
        Statius Albius Oppianicus
             (the Younger)
        m. Auria, d. of Sassia and
           Aulus Aurius Melinus
```

Thus the family consisted of himself and his brother,
who had married the daughter of one of the Aurii.
Accordingly he poisoned both his brother and his
brother's wife.

There remained the third family, the Cluentii,
one of whom, the elder Cluentia, he had already
married and murdered. Their family tree is as
follows:

THE CLUENTII

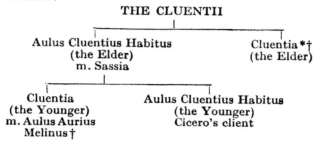

Oppianicus now proceeded to fall in love with his
deceased wife's sister-in-law, Sassia, mother of
Cicero's client and the villainess of our story. He
had been married four times already; but as his
first two wives were dead, his third divorced and
his fourth dead, he was free to marry yet again.
Sassia, twice married, was also free, as her first
husband, Cluentius' father, had died and her
second (who was also her nephew and her son-in-
law!) had been murdered by the intending bride-
groom. But though she did not object to marrying
a widower, she did object to step-sons, of whom
Oppianicus would bring her three. Her objection
was however removed by Oppianicus, who promptly
murdered the two youngest. The marriage was now
able to take place.

There remained, then, of the Cluentii two only—
Sassia's own children, the younger Aulus Cluentius
Habitus and his sister. Cluentius, the hero of our
story, was now head of the family. He was im-
mensely wealthy, besides which Oppianicus dis-
liked him personally; but above all he was known
to have made no will, so that in the event of his
death the whole family property would pass to his
mother Sassia—now married to Oppianicus and
therefore easily removable, when she had inherited,
by a "past-master in the art of wife-murder".

Cluentius, however, was an able, as well as a
wealthy, man; and to murder him was a difficult,
if congenial, task. Oppianicus tried to repeat his
success in Dinaea's case and employed a rascal,
called Fabricius, to corrupt Cluentius' doctor. But
the plot miscarried through the fidelity of a slave;
and Fabricius' freedman, Scamander, was caught in
the act of delivering the poison which was to be
administered to Cluentius. Cluentius might, of
course, have prosecuted Oppianicus at once as
principal; but he thought it wise to proceed first
against his two agents, Fabricius and Scamander.
Both were accordingly put on trial and both were
found guilty.

Cluentius had therefore every reason for confidence in now prosecuting Oppianicus before the
praetor Junius. Oppianicus, having every reason
for despair, decided to bribe the jury. So he employed a notorious crook called Staienus, who,
however, double-crossed him, voted "guilty"

himself and was followed by most of the jury, including the disappointed ones. Some, however,
having heard vague rumours of corruption, preferred to vote "not proven", and five even went
so far as to vote "not guilty". Oppianicus, convicted by a majority, went into exile and died in
two years. Staienus was sued for the bribe which
he had kept to himself and was forced to disgorge.

This ought to have been the end of the story;
and so it might well have been had there not been
those who were determined to carry it on.
Quinctius the tribune, a turbulent demagogue
whom Oppianicus had employed as his counsel,
thought that he could use a judicial scandal as a
stick with which to beat the Senate, whose mem-
bers, at the time of Oppianicus' trial, were the only
people who were allowed to serve on juries. He
therefore spread the rumour that Junius' court had
been bribed, not by Oppianicus, but by Cluentius,
and that an innocent man had fallen a victim to
corruption. It is possible that Cluentius also
bribed the jury (as we gather that he did from
what Cicero said after his trial) but the record of
Oppianicus unfits him for the rôle of injured
innocence.

Sassia, too, was disinclined to let the matter
drop; and on the death of her husband at once
started to mature a plot to accuse her son Cluentius
of having used corruption to secure his step-father's
conviction, and of having afterwards poisoned him.
She purchased from Oppianicus' doctor a slave

called Strato, whom, together with one Nicostratus, a faithful slave of her late husband, she
examined by torture in the presence of witnesses,
with the hope of extracting a confession damaging
to Cluentius. But in vain; the evidence she wanted
was not to be wrung from them, and the inquiry
was dropped.

For three years Sassia held her hand, taking no
further step than to betroth her daughter Auria,
a considerable heiress, to the younger Oppianicus,
so as to get him into her power. She took Strato
back into favour and actually furnished him with
the means to set up in business as a chemist. He ill
repaid her kindness, for he procceded to burgle her
safe, having first committed murder to cover his
tracks. But he was detected through the instrument that he had used for his safe-breaking, and
an inquiry was held.

This gave Sassia her chance. Strato—and
Nicostratus with him—was again put to the torture; and under cover of questioning them upon
this more recent crime, she tried once more to ex-
tract an admission that Cluentius had poisoned her
husband. Once more she failed; and in her ex-
asperation she put Strato to a cruel death. She
then forged his "confession" in the terms she
wanted. All was now ready for her attack on
Cluentius. She forced her step-son Oppianicus to
act as prosecutor and entrusted the brief to a
young advocate named Titus Accius. Cluentius
was defended by Cicero; and this volume contains

the narrative portions of the speech which he then delivered.

It is a brilliant speech, made at a time when Cicero was at the height of his powers and in a cause which aroused his passionate sympathy. Its difficulty will be largely overcome in advance by anyone who takes the trouble to read and to master the story which has been thus briefly told in the Introduction.[1] One point in particular should be borne in mind: that though the occasion of this speech in 66 B.C. was the prosecution of Aulus Cluentius Habitus by Statius Albius Oppianicus the Younger for the murder of his father, Statius Albius Oppianicus the Elder, the speech is mainly concerned with the misdeeds of the elder Oppianicus as revealed at his trial before Junius, when prosecuted by Cluentius in 74 B.C. The fact that the two Oppianici had the same names, and that their rôles and that of Cluentius were reversed at the two trials, must be remembered if confusion is to be avoided.

[1] Those who would care to read a fuller and more vivid presentation of the story are recommended to J. A. Froude's *Short Studies on Great Subjects*, vol. III, where they will find it under the title "Society in Italy in the last days of the Roman Republic". The present writer ventures to disagree with the judgment, and sometimes even with the accuracy, of this delightful essay.

PART I

THE CRIMES OF OPPIANICUS
AND SASSIA

*(1) The ousting of Cluentia. (2) The murder of Marcus
Aurius. (3) The murders of the other Aurii.*

My client's mother Sassia, the source of all his troubles, **1**
began her infamous career by falling in love with her own
son-in-law.

A. Cluentius Habitus fuit, pater huiusce, iudices,
homo non solum municipii Larinatis, ex quo erat,
sed etiam regionis illius et vicinitatis, virtute, existimatione, nobilitate facile princeps. Is cum esset
mortuus, Sulla et Pompeio consulibus, reliquit **5**
hunc annos xv natum, grandem autem et nubilem
filiam: quae brevi tempore post patris mortem
nupsit A. Aurio Melino, consobrino suo, adulescenti
in primis, ut tum habebatur, inter suos et honesto
et nobili. Cum essent hae nuptiae plenae dignitatis, **10**
plenae concordiae, repente est exorta mulieris im-
portunae nefaria libido, non solum dedecore verum
etiam scelere coniuncta. Nam Sassia, mater huius
Habiti—mater enim a me in omni causa, tametsi
in hunc hostili odio et crudelitate est, mater, in- **15**
quam, appellabitur:—ea igitur mater Habiti, Melini
illius adulescentis, generi sui, contra quam fas erat,
amore capta, primo, neque id ipsum diu, quoquo
modo poterat, in illa cupiditate se continebat:
deinde ita flagrare coepit amentia, ut eam non **20**
pudor, non pudicitia, non pietas, non macula
familiae, non hominum fama, non filii dolor, non

1

filiae maeror a cupiditate revocaret. Animum adulescentis, nondum consilio ac ratione firmatum,
25 pellexit iis omnibus rebus, quibus illa aetas capi ac deleniri potest. Filia, quae non solum illo communi dolore muliebri in eiusmodi viri iniuriis angeretur, sed nefarium matris pelicatum ferre non posset, de quo ne queri quidem sine scelere se posse arbitra-
30 retur, ceteros sui tanti mali ignaros esse cupiebat: in huius amantissimi sui fratris manibus et gremio, maerore et lacrimis consenescebat.

2 She induced him to divorce his wife, her own daughter and my client's sister, and then had the effrontery to marry him.

Ecce autem subitum divortium; quod solatium malorum omnium fore videbatur. Discedit a Melino Cluentia; ut in tantis iniuriis, non invita: ut a viro, non libenter. Tum vero illa egregia et prae-
5 clara mater palam exsultare laetitia, ac triumphare gaudio coepit, victrix filiae, non libidinis. Itaque diutius suspicionibus obscuris laedi famam suam noluit: nubit genero socrus, nullis auspicibus, nullis auctoribus, funestis ominibus omnium.
10   O mulieris scelus incredibile, et, praeter hanc unam, in omni vita inauditum! O libidinem effrenatam et indomitam! O audaciam singularem! nonne timuisse, si minus vim deorum, hominumque famam, at illos ipsos parietes, superiorum testes
15 nuptiarum? Perfregit ac prostravit omnia cupiditate ac furore: vicit pudorem libido, timorem audacia, rationem amentia. Tulit hoc commune dedecus iam familiae, cognationis, nominis, graviter

2

filius: augebatur autem eius molestia quotidianis
querimoniis et assiduo fletu sororis.   20

I now turn to the series of crimes for which Oppianicus was **3**
justly condemned eight years ago. He began with Dinaea,
whose sole surviving son, long lost and recently discovered,
he caused to be murdered so as to secure the family property for his own son.

Initium quod huic cum matre fuerit simultatis
audistis. Nunc iam summatim exponam, quibus
criminibus Oppianicus damnatus sit. Atque ut intellegatis iis accusatum esse criminibus Oppianicum, ut neque accusator timere, neque reus sperare 5
potuerit, pauca vobis illius iudicii crimina exponam:
quibus cognitis, nemo vestrum mirabitur, illum,
diffidentem rebus suis, ad Staienum atque ad
pecuniam confugisse.

Larinas quaedam fuit Dinaea, socrus Oppianici: 10
quae filios habuit M. Aurium et Num. Aurium et
Cn. Magium, et filiam Magiam nuptam Oppianico. M. Aurius adulescentulus, bello Italico
captus apud Asculum, in Q. Sergii senatoris, eius,
qui inter sicarios damnatus est, manus incidit, et 15
apud eum fuit in ergastulo. Numerius autem
Aurius, frater eius, mortuus est, heredemque Cn.
Magium fratrem reliquit. Postea Magia, uxor Oppianici, mortua est; postremo unus, qui reliquus
erat, Dinaeae filius, Cn. Magius, est mortuus. Is 20
fecit heredem illum adulescentem Oppianicum,
sororis suae filium, eumque partiri cum Dinaea
matre iussit. Interim venit index ad Dinaeam,
neque obscurus neque incertus, qui nuntiaret ei,

25 filium eius, M. Aurium, vivere, et in agro Gallico
esse in servitute. Mulier, amissis liberis, cum unius
filii recuperandi spes esset ostentata, omnes suos
propinquos filiique sui necessarios convocavit, et
ab iis flens petivit, ut negotium susciperent, adu-
30 lescentem investigarent, sibi restituerent eum
filium, quem tamen unum ex multis fortuna reliquum esse voluisset. Haec cum agere instituisset,
oppressa morbo est. Itaque testamentum fecit
eiusmodi, ut illi filio HS cccc milia legaret, here-
35 dem institueret eundem illum Oppianicum, nepotem
suum. Atque his diebus paucis est mortua. Propin-
qui tamen illi, quemadmodum viva Dinaea institu-
erant, ita, mortua illa, ad vestigandum Aurium cum
eodem illo indice in agrum Gallicum profecti sunt.
40 Interim Oppianicus, ut erat, sicuti multis ex
rebus reperietis, singulari scelere et audacia, per
quendam Gallicanum, familiarem suum, primum
illum indicem pecunia corrupit, deinde ipsum
Aurium, non magna iactura facta, tollendum inter-
45 ficiendumque curavit.

4 Attacked by Dinaea's outraged relatives, Oppianicus fled to
the camp of one of Sulla's generals, from whom he returned
armed with powers to proclaim martial law at Larinum.
He took the opportunity to execute everyone who might
give evidence against him.

Illi autem, qui erant ad propinquum investi-
gandum et recuperandum profecti, litteras Larinum
ad Aurios, illius adulescentis suosque necessarios,
mittunt; sibi difficilem esse investigandi rationem,
5 quod intellegerent indicem ab Oppianico esse cor-

4

ruptum. Quas litteras A. Aurius, vir fortis et experiens, et domi nobilis, M. illius Aurii propinquus,
in foro, palam, multis audientibus, cum adesset
Oppianicus, recitat, et clarissima voce, se nomen
Oppianici, si interfectum M. Aurium comperisset, 10
delaturum esse testatur. Interim brevi tempore
illi, qui erant in agrum Gallicum profecti, Larinum
revertuntur: interfectum esse M. Aurium renunti-
ant. Animi non solum propinquorum, sed etiam
omnium Larinatium odio Oppianici, et illius adu- 15
lescentis misericordia, commoventur. Itaque cum
A. Aurius, is qui antea denuntiarat, clamore
hominem ac minis insequi coepisset, Larino pro-
fugit, et se in castra clarissimi viri, Q. Metelli, contulit. Post illam autem fugam, et sceleris et con- 20
scientiae testem, numquam se iudiciis, numquam
legibus, numquam inermem inimicis committere
ausus est: sed per illam L. Sullae vim atque vic-
toriam, Larinum in summo timore omnium cum
armatis advolavit: quattuorviros, quos municipes 25
fecerant, sustulit: se a Sulla et alios praeterea tres
factos esse dixit: et ab eodem sibi esse imperatum,
ut Aurium illum, qui sibi delationem nominis et
capitis periculum ostentarat, et alterum Aurium,
et eius C. filium, et Sex. Vibium, quo sequestre in 30
illo indice corrumpendo dicebatur esse usus, pro-
scribendos interficiendosque curaret. Itaque, illis
crudelissime interfectis, non mediocri ab eo ceteri
proscriptionis et mortis metu terrebantur. His
rebus in causa iudicioque patefactis, quis est, qui 35
illum absolvi posse arbitraretur?

PART II

THE WOOING OF SASSIA BY OPPIANICUS

(1) *The murder of his own sons.* (2) *The murder of his first wife, Cluentia.* (3) *The murder of his brother, C. Oppianicus.* (4) *The murder of his brother's wife, Auria.* (5) *The murder of the young rake, Asuvius.* (6) *The murder of his mother-in-law, Dinaea.* (7) *The forging of Dinaea's will.*

5 Worse followed. Sassia objected to marrying a man who would bring her three step-sons. So Oppianicus removed her objection by murdering the two youngest—and the marriage took place.

Atque haec parva sunt: cognoscite reliqua: ut non aliquando condemnatum esse Oppianicum, sed aliquamdiu incolumem fuisse miremini.

Primum videte hominis audaciam. Sassiam in
5 matrimonium ducere, Habiti matrem, illam, cuius virum A. Aurium occiderat, concupivit. Utrum impudentior hic, qui postulet, an crudelior illa, si nubat, difficile dictu est. Sed tamen utriusque humanitatem constantiamque cognoscite. Petit
10 Oppianicus, ut sibi Sassia nubat, et id magno opere contendit. Illa autem non admiratur audaciam, non impudentiam aspernatur, non denique illam Oppianici domum, viri sui sanguine redundantem, reformidat: sed quod haberet tres ille filios, idcirco
15 se ab his nuptiis abhorrere respondit. Oppianicus, qui pecuniam Sassiae concupivisset, domo sibi quaerendum remedium existimavit ad eam moram, quae nuptiis afferebatur. Nam cum haberet ex

6

Novia infantem filium, alter autem eius filius, Papia
natus, Teani Apuli, quod abest a Larino XVIII milia 20
passuum, apud matrem educaretur, arcessit subito
sine causa puerum Teano: quod facere, nisi ludis
publicis, aut festis diebus, antea non solebat. Mater
nihil mali misera suspicans mittit. Ille se Tarentum proficisci cum simulasset, eo ipso die puer, cum 25
hora undecima in publico valens visus esset, ante
noctem mortuus, et postridie, antequam luceret,
combustus est. Atque hunc tantum maerorem
matri prius hominum rumor quam quisquam ex
Oppianici familia nuntiavit. Illa, cum uno tempore 30
audisset, sibi non solum filium sed etiam exse-
quiarum munus ereptum, Larinum confestim ex-
animata venit, et ibi de integro funus iam sepulto
filio fecit. Dies nondum decem intercesserant, cum
ille alter filius infans necatur. Itaque nubit Oppi- 35
anico continuo Sassia, laetanti iam animo et spe
optima confirmato. Nec mirum, quae se non
nuptialibus donis, sed filiorum funeribus delenitam
videret. Ita quod ceteri propter liberos pecuniae
cupidiores solent esse, ille propter pecuniam liberos 40
amittere iucundius esse duxit.

You are indignant at this story of crimes now many years 6
old. What must their indignation have been who heard the
story at first hand?

Sentio, iudices, vos pro vestra humanitate, his
tantis sceleribus breviter a me demonstratis, vehementer esse commotos. Quo tandem igitur animo
fuisse illos arbitramini, quibus his de rebus non

5 modo audiendum fuit, verum etiam iudicandum? Vos auditis de eo, in quem iudices non estis: de eo, quem non videtis: de eo, quem odisse iam non potestis: de eo, qui et naturae et legibus satisfecit: quem leges exsilio, natura morte multavit. Auditis
10 non ab inimico: auditis sine testibus: auditis, cum ea, quae copiosissime dici possunt, breviter a me strictimque dicuntur. Illi audiebant de eo, de quo iurati sententias ferre debebant: de eo, cuius praesentis nefarium et consceleratum vultum intue-
15 bantur: de eo, quem oderant propter audaciam: de eo, quem omni supplicio dignum esse ducebant. Audiebant ab accusatoribus: audiebant verba multorum testium: audiebant, cum unaquaque de re a P. Canutio, homine eloquentissimo, graviter
20 et diu diceretur. Et est quisquam, qui, cum haec cognoverit, suspicari possit, Oppianicum iudicio oppressum et circumventum esse innocentem?

7 Oppianicus also poisoned his first wife, his brother's wife and his brother.

Acervatim iam reliqua, iudices, dicam, ut ad ea, quae propiora huius causae et adiunctiora sunt, perveniam. Vos, quaeso, memoria teneatis, non mihi hoc esse propositum, ut accusem Oppianicum
5 mortuum; sed, cum hoc persuadere vobis velim, iudicium ab hoc non esse corruptum, hoc uti initio ac fundamento defensionis, Oppianicum, hominem sceleratissimum et nocentissimum, esse damnatum. Qui uxori suae Cluentiae, quae amita huius Habiti
10 fuit, cum ipse poculum dedisset, subito illa in media

potione exclamavit, se maximo cum dolore mori:
nec diutius vixit, quam locuta est: nam in ipso
sermone hoc et vociferatione mortua est. Et ad
hanc mortem tam repentinam, vocemque morientis,
omnia praeterea, quae solent esse indicia et vestigia 15
veneni, in illius mortuae corpore fuerunt.

Eodemque veneno C. Oppianicum fratrem necavit. Neque est hoc satis: tametsi in ipso fraterno
parricidio nullum scelus praetermissum videtur;
tamen, ut ad hoc nefarium facinus accederet, adi- 20
tum sibi aliis sceleribus ante munivit. Nam cum
esset gravida Auria, fratris uxor, et iam appropinquare partus videretur, mulierem veneno inter-
fecit. Post fratrem aggressus est: qui sero, iam
exhausto illo poculo mortis, cum et de suo et de 25
uxoris interitu clamaret, testamentumque mutare
cuperet, in ipsa significatione huius voluntatis est
mortuus.

Again, there was the murder of the young rake, Asuvius, and 8
the forging of his will.

Quid? illa caedes Asuvii Larinatis, adulescentis
pecuniosi, quam clara tum, recenti re, fuit, quam
omnium sermone celebrata! Fuit Avillius quidam
Larinas perdita nequitia et summa egestate, arte
quadam praeditus, ad libidines adulescentulorum 5
excitandas accommodatus: qui ut se blanditiis et
assentationibus in Asuvii consuetudinem penitus
immersit, Oppianicus continuo sperare coepit, hoc
se Avillio, tamquam aliqua machina admota,
capere Asuvii adulescentiam, et fortunas eius patrias 10

9

expugnare posse. Ratio excogitata Larini est: res translata Romam. Inire enim id consilium facilius solitudine, perficere rem eiusmodi commodius in turba posse arbitrati sunt. Asuvius cum Avillio 15 Romam est profectus. Hos vestigiis Oppianicus consecutus est. Iam ut Romae vixerint, quibus conviviis, quibus flagitiis, quantis et quam profusis sumptibus, non modo conscio, sed etiam conviva et adiutore Oppianico, longum est mihi dicere, 20 praesertim ad alia properanti. Exitum huius assimulatae familiaritatis cognoscite. Cum esset adulescens apud sodalem quendam atque, ubi pernoctaret, ibi diem posterum commoraretur, Avillius, ut erat constitutum, simulat se aegrotare, 25 et testamentum facere velle. Oppianicus obsignatores ad eum, qui neque Asuvium, neque Avillium nossent, adducit, et illum Asuvium appellat: ipse, testamento Asuvii nomine obsignato, discedit. Avillius illico convalescit. Asuvius autem brevi illo 30 tempore, quasi in hortulos iret, in harenarias quasdam extra portam Esquilinam perductus, occiditur.

9 The friends of Asuvius, finding his corpse, haled Oppianicus before the judgment-seat of Manlius. But there was a "business deal"; and—you know Manlius—the case was dropped.

Qui cum unum iam et alterum diem desideraretur, neque in iis locis, ubi ex consuetudine quaerebatur, inveniretur, et Oppianicus in foro Larinatium dictitaret, nuper se et suos amicos

testamentum eius obsignasse; liberti Asuvii, et 5
nonnulli amici, quod eo die, quo postremum
Asuvius visus erat, Avillium cum eo fuisse, et a
multis visum esse constabat, in eum invadunt et
hominem ante pedes Q. Manlii, qui tum erat triumvir, constituunt. Atque ille continuo, nullo teste, 10
nullo indice, recentis maleficii conscientia perterritus, omnia, ut a me paullo ante dicta sunt, ex-
ponit, Asuviumque ab se, consilio Oppianici, interfectum fatetur. Extrahitur domo latitans Oppianicus a Manlio: index Avillius ex altera parte 15
coram tenetur. Hic iam quid reliqua quaeritis?
Manlium plerique noratis. Non ille honorem a
pueritia, non studia virtutis, non ullum existima-
tionis bonae fructum umquam cogitarat: sed ex
petulanti atque improbo scurra, in discordiis civi- 20
tatis ad eam columnam, ad quam multorum saepe
conviciis perductus erat, tum suffragiis populi per-
venerat. Itaque rem cum Oppianico transigit:
pecuniam ab eo accipit: causam et susceptam et
manifestam relinquit. Ac tum in Oppianici causa, 25
crimen hoc Asuvianum cum testibus multis, tum
vero indicio Avillii probabatur: in quo alligatum
Oppianici nomen primum esse constabat, eius,
quem vos miserum atque innocentem falso iudicio
circumventum esse dicitis.   30

Finally, there was the murder of Dinaea by means of the quack **10**
doctor, the forging of her will and of the public records.

   Quid? aviam tuam, Oppianice, Dinaeam, cui tu
es heres, pater tuus non manifesto necavit? ad

quam cum adduxisset medicum illum suum, iam cognitum et saepe victorem, mulier exclamat, se
5 ab eo nullo modo velle curari, quo curante suos omnes perdidisset. Tum repente Anconitanum quendam, L. Clodium, pharmacopolam circumforaneum, qui casu tum Larinum venisset, aggreditur, et cum eo duobus milibus HS, id quod ipsius
10 tabulis tum est demonstratum, transigit. L. Clodius, qui properaret, cui fora multa restarent, simul atque introductus est, rem confecit: prima potione mulierem sustulit: neque postea Larini punctum est temporis commoratus. Eadem hac
15 Dinaea testamentum faciente, cum tabulas prehendisset Oppianicus, qui gener eius fuisset, digito legata delevit: et, cum id multis locis fecisset, post mortem eius, ne lituris coargui posset, testamentum in alias tabulas transcriptum, signis adulterinis
20 obsignavit. Multa praetereo consulto. Etenim vereor, ne haec ipsa nimium multa esse videantur. Vos tamen eum similem sui fuisse in ceteris vitae partibus existimare debetis. Illum tabulas publicas Larini censorias corrupisse, decuriones universi
25 iudicaverunt.

11 Small wonder that no one would have any social or business dealings with Oppianicus. But guilty though he was, my client would never have prosecuted him except to save his own life.

Cum illo iam nemo rationem, nemo rem ullam contrahebat: nemo illum ex tam multis cognatis et affinibus tutorem umquam liberis suis scripsit:

12

nemo illum aditu, nemo congressione, nemo sermone, nemo convivio dignum iudicabat: omnes 5
aspernabantur, omnes abhorrebant, omnes, ut ali-
quam immanem ac perniciosam bestiam pestemque
fugiebant. Hunc tamen hominem tam audacem,
tam nefarium, tam nocentem, numquam accusasset
Habitus, iudices, si id praetermittere, salvo capite 10
suo, potuisset. Erat huic inimicus Oppianicus:
erat: sed tamen erat vitricus: crudelis et huic in-
festa mater: attamen mater. Postremo nihil tam
remotum ab accusatione quam Cluentius, et
natura, et voluntate, et instituta ratione vitae. 15
Sed cum esset haec illi proposita conditio, ut aut
iuste pieque accusaret, aut acerbe indigneque
moreretur; accusare, quoquo modo posset, quam
illo modo emori, maluit.

PART III
ATTEMPT OF OPPIANICUS TO
MURDER CLUENTIUS: TRIAL
OF HIS AGENTS

12 Cluentius was known to have made no will: and this was enough to mark him out as a victim for Oppianicus.

Atque, ut haec ita esse perspicere possitis, exponam vobis Oppianici facinus manifesto compertum atque deprehensum: ex quo simul utrumque, et huic accusare, et illi condemnari, necesse 5 fuisse intellegetis. Nam Habitus, usque ad illius iudicii tempus, nullum testamentum umquam fecerat. Neque enim legare eiusmodi matri poterat animum inducere, neque testamento nomen omnino praetermittere parentis. Id cum Oppi- 10 anicus sciret (neque enim erat obscurum), intellegebat, Habito mortuo, bona eius omnia ad matrem esse ventura: quae ab sese postea, aucta pecunia maiore praemio, orbata filio minore periculo, necaretur. Itaque his rebus incensus, 15 qua ratione Habitum veneno tollere conatus sit, cognoscite.

13 Oppianicus selected as his agent a rascal called Fabricius; but the plot was discovered through the fidelity of a slave, a trap was set and Fabricius' freedman, Scamander, was caught with the poison for Cluentius upon him.

C. et L. Fabricii fratres gemini fuerunt ex municipio Aletrinati, homines inter se cum forma tum moribus similes, municipum autem suorum dissimillimi: in quibus quantus splendor sit, quam

prope aequabilis, quam fere omnium constans et 5
moderata ratio vitae, nemo vestrum, ut mea fert
opinio, ignorat. His Fabriciis semper usus est
Oppianicus familiarissime. Iam hoc fere scitis
omnes, quantam vim habeat ad coniungendas ami-
citias studiorum ac naturae similitudo. Cum illi ita 10
viverent ut nullum quaestum turpem esse arbitra-
rentur; cum omnis ab his fraus, omnes insidiae
circumscriptionesque adulescentium nascerentur;
cumque essent vitiis atque improbitate omnibus
noti; studiose, ut dixi, ad eorum se familiaritatem 15
multis iam ante annis Oppianicus applicarat.
Itaque tum sic statuit, per C. Fabricium (nam L.
erat mortuus) insidias Habito comparare. Erat illo
tempore infirma valetudine Habitus. Utebatur
autem medico non ignobili, sed spectato homine, 20
Cleophanto: cuius servum Diogenem Fabricius ad
venenum Habito dandum spe et pretio sollicitare
coepit. Servus non incallidus, sed, ut ipsa res de-
claravit, frugi atque integer, sermonem Fabricii
non est aspernatus: rem ad dominum detulit: 25
Cleophantus autem cum Habito est locutus.
Habitus statim cum M. Baebio senatore, famili-
arissimo suo, communicavit: qui qua fide, qua
prudentia, qua dignitate fuerit, meminisse vos
arbitror. Ei placuit, ut Diogenem Habitus emeret 30
a Cleophanto, quo facilius aut comprehenderetur
res eius indicio, aut falsa esse cognosceretur. Ne
multis. Diogenes emitur: venenum diebus paucis
comparatur: multi viri boni cum ex occulto inter-
venissent, pecunia obsignata, quae ad eam rem da- 35

15

batur, in manibus Scamandri, liberti Fabriciorum,
deprehenditur. Pro di immortales! Oppianicum
quisquam, his rebus cognitis, circumventum esse
dicet? simul et illud quis est qui dubitet, quin, hac
40 re comperta manifestoque deprehensa, aut ob-
eunda mors Cluentio, aut suscipienda accusatio
fuerit?

14 Cluentius decided to establish the case against Oppianicus
by first putting his agents on trial. Accordingly Scamander
was tried and convicted.

Satis esse arbitror demonstratum, iudices, iis criminibus accusatum esse Oppianicum, ut honeste
absolvi nullo modo potuerit. Cognoscite nunc ita
reum citatum esse illum ut, re semel atque iterum
5 praeiudicata, condemnatus in iudicium venerit.
Nam Cluentius, iudices, primum nomen eius detulit, cuius in manibus venenum deprehenderat.
Is erat libertus Fabriciorum, Scamander. Integrum
consilium: iudicii corrupti nulla suspicio: simplex
10 in iudicium causa, certa res, unum crimen allatum
est. Itum est in consilium. Omnibus sententiis,
praeter unam quam suam Staienus esse dicebat,
Scamander prima actione condemnatus est. Quis
tum erat omnium, qui, Scamandro condemnato,
15 non iudicium de Oppianico factum esse arbitraretur? quid est illa damnatione iudicatum, nisi
venenum id, quod Habito daretur, esse quaesitum?
Quae porro tenuissima suspicio collata in Scamandrum est, aut conferri potuit, ut is sua sponte
20 necare voluisse Habitum putaretur?

The trial of Fabricius followed. His counsel was doing his **15**
poor best, but Fabricius, without waiting for the verdict,
condemned himself by bolting from the court.

Atque hoc tum iudicio facto, et Oppianico, re et
existimatione iam, lege et pronuntiatione nondum,
condemnato, tamen Habitus Oppianicum reum
statim non fecit. Voluit cognoscere, utrum iudices
in eos solos essent severi, quos venenum habuisse 5
ipsos comperissent, an etiam consilia conscientiasque eiusmodi facinorum supplicio dignas
iudicarent. Itaque C. Fabricium, quem propter
familiaritatem Oppianici conscium illi facinori
fuisse arbitrabatur, reum statim fecit. Hic tum 10
Fabricius inopia et necessitate coactus, in causa
eiusmodi ad Caepasios fratres confugit, homines
industrios, atque eo animo, ut quaecunque dicendi
potestas esset data, in honore atque in beneficio
ponerent. 15
Citatur reus: agitur causa: paucis verbis accusat,
ut de re iudicata, Canutius. Incipit longo et alte
petito prooemio respondere maior Caepasius.
Primo attente auditur eius oratio. Erigebat animum iam demissum et oppressum Oppianicus. 20
Gaudebat ipse Fabricius. Non intellegebat, animos
iudicum non illius eloquentia sed defensionis impudentia commoveri. Posteaquam de re coepit
dicere, ad ea, quae erant in causa, addebat etiam
ipse nova quaedam vulnera: ut, quamquam sedulo 25
faciebat, tamen interdum non defendere sed praevaricari accusationi videretur. Itaque cum calli-
dissime se dicere putaret, et cum illa verba gravis-

17

sima ex intimo artificio deprompsisset: *Respicite,*
30 *iudices, hominum fortunas, respicite dubios variosque*
casus, respicite C. Fabricii senectutem; cum hoc,
Respicite, ornandae orationis causa saepe dixisset,
respexit ipse; at C. Fabricius a subselliis, demisso
capite, discesserat. Hic iudices ridere: stomachari
35 atque acerbe ferre patronus, causam sibi eripi, et
se cetera de illo loco, *Respicite iudices,* non posse
dicere: nec quicquam propius est factum quam ut
illum persequeretur, et collo obtorto ad subsellia
reduceret, ut reliqua posset perorare. Ita tum
40 Fabricius, primum suo iudicio, quod est gravis-
simum, deinde legis vi et sententiis iudicum est
condemnatus.

16 These two verdicts made the conviction of Oppianicus
inevitable. How could the principal hope to be acquitted
by the same court that had already convicted his agents?

Quid est, quod iam de Oppianici causa plura
dicamus? Apud eosdem iudices reus est factus,
cum his duobus praeiudiciis iam damnatus esset:
accusatus est criminibus gravissimis, et iis, quae a
5 me breviter dicta sunt, et praeterea multis quae
ego omnia nunc omitto: accusatus est apud eos,
qui Scamandrum, ministrum Oppianici, Fabricium,
conscium maleficii, condemnarant. Quid enim tandem illi iudices responderent, si quis ab iis quae-
10 reret: Condemnastis Scamandrum: quo crimine?
Nempe quod Habitum, per servum medici, veneno
necare voluisset. Quid Habiti morte Scamander
consequebatur? Nihil: sed administer erat Oppi-

anici. Condemnastis C. Fabricium. Quid ita? Quia, cum ipse familiarissime Oppianico usus, libertus 15 autem eius in maleficio deprehensus esset, illum expertem eius consilii fuisse non probabatur. Si igitur ipsum Oppianicum, bis suis iudiciis condemnatum, absolvissent, quis tantam turpitudinem iudiciorum, quis tantam inconstantiam rerum 20 iudicatarum, quis tantam libidinem iudicum ferre potuisset?

PART IV
THE TRIAL OF OPPIANICUS.
WHO BRIBED THE JURY?

17 Oppianicus was convicted in his turn, not through bribery, but on the evidence. He may well have tried bribery himself—and actually did so, through the agency of Staienus. Who dares deny it?

Quod si hoc videtis, quod iam hac omni oratione patefactum est, illo iudicio reum condemnari praesertim ab iisdem iudicibus, qui duo praeiudicia fecissent, necesse fuisse, simul illud videatis
5 necesse est, nullam accusatori causam esse potuisse, cur iudicium vellet corrumpere. Atque ego illa non argumentabor, quae sunt gravia vehementer: eum corrupisse, qui in periculo fuerit: eum, qui metuerit: eum, qui spem salutis in alia ratione non
10 habuerit: eum, qui semper singulari fuerit audacia. Multa sunt eiusmodi. Verum cum habeam rem non dubiam, sed apertam atque manifestam, enumeratio singulorum argumentorum non est necessaria.
15 Dico, C. Aelio Staieno, iudici, pecuniam grandem Statium Albium ad corrumpendum iudicium dedisse. Num quis negat? Te appello, Oppianice, te, T. Acci: quorum alter eloquentia damnationem illam, alter tacita pietate deplorat. Audete negare,
20 ab Oppianico Staieno iudici pecuniam datam: negate, negate, inquam, in eo loco. Quid reticetis? At negare non potestis, quod repetistis, quod confessi estis, quod abstulistis. Quo tandem igitur ore mentionem corrupti iudicii facitis, cum ab ista

parte iudici pecuniam ante iudicium datam, post 25
iudicium ereptam esse fateamini?

We know the details of the transaction. Oppianicus, in **18**
desperation, approached Staienus, an old hand at the game.
Staienus bargained for 640,000 sesterces to be distributed
among his fellow jurymen, but secretly determined to keep
it all to himself.

Quonam igitur haec modo gesta sunt? Repetam
paullo altius, iudices, et omnia, quae in diuturna
obscuritate latuerunt, sic aperiam, ut ea cernere
oculis videamini. Vos, quaeso, ut adhuc me attente
audistis, item, quae reliqua sunt, audiatis: pro- 5
fecto nihil a me dicetur, quod non dignum hoc conventu et silentio, dignum vestris studiis atque
auribus esse videatur.

Nam, ut primum Oppianicus, ex eo, quod
Scamander reus erat factus, quid sibi impenderet, 10
coepit suspicari, statim se ad hominis egentis,
audacis, in iudiciis corrumpendis exercitati, tum
autem iudicis, Staieni familiaritatem applicavit.
Ac primum Scamandro reo tantum datis muneri-
bus perfecerat, ut eo fautore uteretur cupidiore 15
quam fides iudicis postulabat. Post autem, cum
esset Scamander unius Staieni sententia absolutus,
patronus autem Scamandri ne sua quidem sententia liberatus, acrioribus saluti suae remediis
subveniendum putavit. Tum a Staieno, sicut ab 20
homine ad excogitandum acutissimo, ad auden-
dum impudentissimo, ad efficiendum acerrimo
(haec enim ille et aliqua ex parte habebat, et
maiore ex parte se habere simulabat), auxilium

25 capiti ac fortunis suis petere coepit, atque orare
hominem ut sibi rationem ostenderet iudicii corrumpendi. Ille autem, quem ad modum ex ipso
Oppianico postea est auditum, negavit quemquam
esse in civitate praeter se qui id efficere possit. Sed
30 primo gravari coepit, quod aedilitatem se petere
cum hominibus nobilissimis et invidiam atque
offensionem timere dicebat; post exoratus initio
permagnam pecuniam poposcit; deinde ad id per-
venit quod confici potuit, HS sescenta quadraginta
35 milia deferri ad se domum iussit. Quae pecunia
simul atque ad eum delata est, homo impurissimus
statim coepit in eiusmodi mente et cogitatione
versari, nihil esse suis rationibus utilius quam
Oppianicum condemnari; illo absoluto pecuniam
40 illam aut iudicibus dispertiendam aut ipsi esse
reddendam; damnato repetiturum esse neminem.
Itaque rem excogitat singularem. Atque haec,
iudices, quae vera dicuntur a nobis, facilius cre-
detis si cum animis vestris longo intervallo recor-
45 dari C. Staieni vitam et naturam volueritis. Nam
perinde ut opinio est de cuiusque moribus, ita,
quid ab eo factum et non factum sit, existimari
potest.

19 Staienus knew his men; and held out tempting promises to
that oddly named pair, Bulbus and Gutta, and, through
them, to the others.

Cum esset egens, sumptuosus, audax, callidus,
perfidiosus, et cum domi suae, miserrimis in locis
et inanissimis, tantum nummorum positum videret,

ad omnem malitiam et fraudem versare mentem
suam coepit: Demne iudicibus? mihi igitur ipsi, 5
praeter periculum et infamiam, quid quaeretur?
nihil excogitem, quamobrem Oppianico damnari
necesse sit? quid tandem? nihil enim est, quod fieri
non possit. Si quis eum forte casus ex periculo eri-
puerit, nonne reddendum est? Praecipitantem 10
igitur impellamus, inquit, et perditum prosterna-
mus. Capit hoc consilium, ut pecuniam quibus-
dam iudicibus levissimis polliceatur: deinde eam
postea supprimat: ut, quoniam graves homines sua
sponte severe iudicaturos putabat, eos qui leviores 15
erant, destitutione iratos Oppianico redderet.
Itaque, ut erat semper praeposterus atque perversus, initium facit a Bulbo: et eum, quod iamdiu
nihil quaesierat, tristem atque oscitantem, leviter
impellit. "Quid tu?" inquit; "ecquid me adiuvas, 20
Bulbe, ne gratis rei publicae serviamus?" Ille vero,
simul atque hoc audivit *ne gratis*, "quo voles",
inquit, "sequar. Sed quid affers?" Tum ei quadraginta milia, si esset absolutus Oppianicus, pol-
licetur: et eum, ut ceteros appellet, quibuscum 25
loqui consuesset, rogat: atque etiam ipse conditor
totius negotii Guttam aspergit huic Bulbo. Itaque
minime amarus iis visus est qui aliquid ex eius sermone speculae degustarant.

But when they wanted to see the colour of their money, he 20
pretended that he could not get it out of Oppianicus.

Unus et alter dies intercesserat, cum res parum
certa videbatur: sequester et confirmator pecuniae

desiderabatur. Tum appellat hilaro vultu hominem
Bulbus, ut blandissime potest: "Quid tu", inquit,
5 "Paete?" (hoc enim sibi Staienus cognomen ex
imaginibus Aeliorum delegerat ne, si se Ligurem
fecisset, nationis magis suae quam generis uti cog-
nomine videretur); "qua de re mecum locutus es,
quaerunt a me ubi sit pecunia". Hic ille planus
10 improbissimus, quaestu iudiciario pastus, qui illi
pecuniae, quam condiderat, spe iam atque animo
incubaret, contrahit frontem (recordamini faciem,
atque illos eius fictos simulatosque vultus!): queri-
tur se ab Oppianico destitutum: et, qui esset totus
15 ex fraude et mendacio factus, quique ea vitia, quae
a natura habebat, etiam studio atque artificio quodam malitiae condivisset, pulchre asseverat se ab
Oppianico destitutum: atque hoc addit testimonii,
sua illum sententia, cum palam omnes laturi es-
20 sent, condemnatum iri.

21 Rumours of attempted bribery now began to leak out.
Oppianicus, counting on sixteen votes at least, was con-
fident of acquittal. Staienus was not in court when the jury
rose to consider their verdict, but Quinctius hauled him
back.

Manarat sermo in consilio, pecuniae quandam
mentionem inter iudices esse versatam. Res neque
tam fuerat occulta quam erat occultanda: neque
tam erat aperta quam rei publicae causa aperienda.
5 In ea obscuritate ac dubitatione omnium, Canutio,
perito homini, qui quodam odore suspicionis
Staienum corruptum esse sensisset, neque dum rem
perfectam arbitraretur, placuit repente pronun-

tiari: DIXERUNT. Hic tum Oppianicus non magno
opere pertimuit. Rem a Staieno perfectam esse 10
arbitrabatur. In consilium erant ituri iudices XXXII;
sententiis XVI absolutio confici poterat. Quadragena
milia nummum in singulos iudices distributa eum
numerum sententiarum conficere debebant, ut ad
cumulum, spe maiorum praemiorum, ipsius Staieni 15
sententia septima decima accederet. Atque etiam
casu tum, quod illud repente erat factum, Staienus
ipse non aderat. Causam nescio quam apud iudicem
defendebat. Facile hoc Habitus patiebatur: facile
Canutius: at non Oppianicus, neque patronus eius 20
L. Quinctius: qui cum esset eo tempore tribunus
plebis, convicium C. Iunio, iudici quaestionis,
maximum fecit, VT NE SINE AELIO IN CONSILIVM
IRETVR: cumque id ei per viatores consulto neglegentius agi videretur, ipse e publico iudicio ad 25
privatum Staieni iudicium profectus est, et illud
pro potestate dimitti iussit: Staienum ipse ad subsellia adduxit.

At the prisoner's request the jury, some angry and all 22
suspicious, voted openly. To everyone's amazement the
venal jurors, who voted first, all voted "guilty". Completely confused, some honest men thereupon voted "not
proven" and some, actually, "not guilty".

Consurgitur in consilium, cum sententias Oppianicus, quae tum erat potestas, palam ferri velle
dixisset, ut Staienus scire posset, quid cuique de-
beretur. Varia iudicum genera: nummarii pauci:
sed omnes irati. Ut qui accipere in campo con- 5
suerunt, iis candidatis, quorum nummos suppressos

esse putant, inimicissimi solent esse, sic eiusmodi
iudices infesti tum reo venerant. Ceteri nocentissimum esse arbitrabantur: sed exspectabant sen-
10 tentias eorum, quos corruptos putabant, ut ex iis
constituerent, a quo iudicium corruptum videretur.
Ecce tibi eiusmodi sortitio, ut in primis Bulbo
et Staieno et Guttae esset iudicandum. Summa
omnium exspectatio, quidnam sententiae ferrent
15 leves ac nummarii iudices. Atque illi omnes sine
ulla dubitatione condemnant. Hic tum iniectus est
hominibus scrupulus et quaedam dubitatio, quidnam esset actum. Deinde homines sapientes, et ex
vetere illa disciplina iudiciorum, qui neque ab-
20 solvere hominem nocentissimum possent, neque
eum, de quo esset orta suspicio, pecunia oppugnatum, re illa incognita, primo condemnare vellent,
NON LIQVERE dixerunt. Nonnulli autem severi
homines, qui hoc statuerunt, quo quisque animo
25 quid fecerit, spectari oportere, etsi alii pecunia ac-
cepta verum iudicarent, tamen nihilo minus se
superioribus suis iudiciis constare putabant oportere. Itaque damnarunt. Quinque omnino fuerunt,
qui illum vestrum innocentem Oppianicum sive
30 imprudentia, sive misericordia, sive aliqua suspicione, sive ambitione adducti, absolverunt.

23 Staienus was afterwards sued for the money and forced
to repay it.

Atque illo ipso tempore in aedes T. Annii,
hominis honestissimi, necessarii et amici mei, noctu
Staienus, arcessitus ab Oppianico, venit. Iam

cetera nota sunt omnibus: ut cum illo Oppianicus
egerit de pecunia: ut ille se redditurum esse dixerit: 5
ut eorum sermonem omnem audierint viri boni,
qui tum consulto propter in occulto stetissent: ut
res patefacta atque in forum prolata, et pecunia
omnis a Staieno extorta atque erepta sit.

**We know, then, that the court was bribed. Was it Cluentius 24
or Oppianicus who bribed it?**

Versatam esse in iudicio pecuniam, constat: ea
quaeritur, unde profecta sit, ab accusatore, an ab
reo? Accusator dicit haec: "Primum, gravissimis
criminibus accusabam, ut nihil opus esset pecunia:
deinde, condemnatum adducebam, ut ne eripi qui- 5
dem pecunia posset: postremo, etiam si absolutus
esset, mearum tamen omnium fortunarum status
incolumis maneret". Quid contra reus? "Primum,
ipsam multitudinem et atrocitatem criminum per-
timescebam: deinde, Fabriciis propter conscientiam 10
mei sceleris condemnatis, me esse condemnatum
sentiebam: postremo, in eum casum veneram, ut
omnis mearum fortunarum status unius iudicii
periculo contineretur."

**Motive, the evidence of his accounts, his behaviour during 25
the trial, the very figures of the sum involved—all point
to Oppianicus alone.**

Age, quoniam corrumpendi iudicii causas ille
multas et graves habuit, hic nullam, profectio
ipsius pecuniae requiratur. Confecit tabulas dili-
gentissime Cluentius. Haec autem res habet hoc

27

5 certe, ut nihil possit neque additum neque de-
tractum de re familiari latere. Anni sunt octo, cum
ista causa in ista meditatione versatur, cum omnia,
quae ad eam rem pertinent, et ex huius et ex
aliorum tabulis agitatis, tractatis, inquiritis: cum
10 interea Cluentianae pecuniae vestigium nullum in-
venitis. Quid? Albiana pecunia vestigiisne nobis
odoranda est, an ad ipsum cubile, vobis ducibus,
venire possumus? Tenentur uno in loco HS $\overline{\text{IↃCXL}}$:
tenentur apud hominem audacissimum: tenentur
15 apud iudicem. Quid vultis amplius?—At enim
Staienus non fuit ab Oppianico, sed a Cluentio ad
iudicium corrumpendum constitutus.—Cur eum,
cum in consilium iretur, Cluentius et Canutius
abesse patiebantur? cur, cum in consilium mitte-
20 bant, Staienum iudicem, cui pecuniam dederant,
non requirebant? Oppianicus quaerebat: Quinctius
flagitabat: sine Staieno ne in consilium iretur,
tribunicia potestate perfectum est.—At condem-
navit.—Hanc enim damnationem dederat obsidem
25 Bulbo et ceteris, ut destitutus ab Oppianico videretur. Sed quid ego haec pluribus, quasi de re
obscura, disputem, cum ipsa pecunia, quae
Staieno data est, numero ac summa sua non modo
quanta fuerit, sed etiam ad quam rem fuerit,
30 ostendat? Sedecim dico iudices, ut Oppianicus
absolveretur, corrumpendos fuisse: ad Staienum
sexcenta et quadraginta milia nummum esse
delata. Si, ut tu dicis, gratiae conciliandae
causa, quadraginta istorum accessio milium
35 quid valet? sin, ut nos dicimus, ut quadragena

milia nummum sedecim iudicibus darentur, non
Archimedes melius potuit discribere. Quare si
istinc causa corrumpendi iudicii, istinc pecunia,
istinc Staienus, istinc denique omnis fraus et audacia est: hinc pudor, honesta vita, nulla suspicio 40
pecuniae, nulla corrumpendi iudicii causa: patimini, veritate patefacta, atque omni errore sublato,
eo transire illius turpitudinis infamiam, ubi cetera
maleficia consistunt: ab eo invidiam discedere aliquando, ad quem numquam accessisse culpam 45
videtis.

PART V
THE CHARGE AGAINST CLUENTIUS.
WHO KILLED OPPIANICUS?

26 It remains for me to answer the charge that my client attempted to poison the younger Oppianicus at his wedding, but poisoned Balbutius by mistake—a highly improbable story. Balbutius died a natural death, as his own father will testify.

Quare quid est praeterea quod in causa relinquatur? Veneficii crimen: Oppianico huic adulescenti, cum eius in nuptiis, more Larinatium, multitudo hominum pranderet, venenum Habiti consilio
5 paratum; id cum daretur in mulso, Balbutium quendam, eius familiarem, intercepisse, bibisse, statimque esse mortuum. Hoc ego si sic agerem tamquam mihi crimen esset diluendum, haec pluribus verbis dicerem, quae nunc paucis percurrit oratio
10 mea. Quid umquam Habitus in se admisit, ut hoc tantum ab eo facinus non abhorrere videatur? quid autem magno opere Oppianicum metuebat, cum ille verbum omnino in hac ipsa causa facere nullum potuerit; huic autem accusatores, matre viva,
15 deesse non possent? quod iam intellegetis. An ut de causa eius periculi nihil decederet, ad causam novum crimen accederet? Quod autem tempus veneni dandi illo die, in illa frequentia? per quem porro datum? unde sumptum? quae deinde inter-
20 ceptio poculi? cur non de integro autem datum? Multa sunt, quae dici possunt: sed non committam ut videar non dicendo voluisse dicere. Res enim iam se ipsa defendit. Nego, illum adulescentem,

quem statim epoto poculo mortuum esse dixistis, omnino illo die esse mortuum. Magnum et im- 25 pudens mendacium! Perspicite cetera. Dico illum, cum ad illud prandium crudior venisset, et, ut aetas illa fert, sibi tamen non pepercisset, aliquot dies aegrotasse, et ita esse mortuum. Quis huic rei testis est? Idem, qui sui luctus, pater: pater, in- 30 quam, illius adulescentis: quem, propter animi dolorem, pertenuis suspicio potuisset ex illo loco testem in A. Cluentium constituere, is hunc suo testimonio sublevat. Quod recita. Tu autem, nisi molestum est, paullisper exsurge, perfer hunc 35 dolorem commemorationis necessariae: in qua ego diutius non morabor, quoniam, quod fuit viri op- timi, fecisti, ut ne cui innocenti maeror tuus cala- mitatem et falsum crimen afferret. [TESTIMONIUM BALBUTII PATRIS.] 40

One last charge my client has to answer—the product of 27 his mother's spite—that he poisoned the elder Oppianicus. What motive had he? What had he to fear? Was it revenge? Then he would have wished to keep the wretched Oppianicus alive!

Unum etiam mihi reliquum eiusmodi crimen est, iudices, ex quo illud perspicere possitis, quod a me initio orationis meae dictum est: quidquid mali per hos annos A. Cluentius viderit, quidquid hoc tem- pore habeat sollicitudinis ac negotii, id omne a 5 matre esse conflatum. Oppianicum veneno ne- catum esse, quod ei datum sit in pane per M. Asellium quendam, familiarem ipsius, idque Habiti consilio factum esse, dicitis. In quo primum illud

10 quaero, quae causa Habito fuerit, cur interficere
Oppianicum vellet. Inimicitias enim inter ipsos
fuisse confiteor: sed homines inimicos suos morte
affici volunt, aut quod metuunt, aut quod oderunt.
Quo tandem igitur Habitus metu adductus, tan-
15 tum in se facinus suscipere conatus est? quid erat,
quod iam Oppianicum poena affectum pro male-
ficiis, eiectum e civitate, quisquam timeret? quid
metuebat? ne oppugnaretur a perdito? an ne ac-
cusaretur a condemnato? an ne exsulis testimonio
20 laederetur? Sin autem, quod oderat Habitus ini-
micum, idcirco illum vita frui noluit, adeone erat
stultus, ut illam, quam tum ille vivebat, vitam
esse arbitraretur, damnati, exsulis, deserti ab
omnibus? quem propter animi importunitatem
25 nemo recipere tecto, nemo adire, nemo alloqui,
nemo aspicere vellet? Huius igitur vitae Habitus
invidebat? Hunc si acerbe et penitus oderat, non
eum quam diutissime vivere velle debebat? huic
mortem maturabat inimicus, quod illi unum in
30 malis perfugium erat calamitatis? Qui si quid animi
et virtutis habuisset (ut multi saepe fortes viri in
eiusmodi dolore), mortem sibi ipse conscisset, huic
quamobrem id vellet inimicus offerre, quod ipse
sibi optare deberet? Nam nunc quidem quid tan-
35 dem illi mali mors attulit? Nisi forte ineptiis ac
fabulis ducimur, ut existimemus illum apud inferos
impiorum supplicia perferre, ac plures illic offendisse inimicos quam hic reliquisse: a socrus, ab
uxorum, a fratris, a liberum Poenis actum esse
40 praecipitem in sceleratorum sedem atque regionem.

Quae si falsa sunt, id quod omnes intellegunt, quid
ei tandem aliud mors eripuit praeter sensum
doloris?

The story does not bear examination: both the agent and **28**
the medium used for administering the poison are most
unlikely. If Oppianicus was murdered, you must look
elsewhere for the murderer.

Age vero, venenum per quem datum? Per M.
Asellium. Quid huic cum Habito? Nihil: atque
adeo, quod ille Oppianico familiarissime est usus,
potius etiam simultas. Eine igitur quem sibi of-
fensiorem Oppianico familiarissimum sciebat esse, 5
potissimum et suum scelus et illius periculum
committebat? Cur deinde tu, qui pietate ad ac-
cusandum excitatus es, hunc Asellium esse inultum
tamdiu sinis? Cur non Habiti exemplo usus es, ut
per illum, qui attulisset venenum, de hoc praeiu- 10
dicaretur? Iam vero illud quam non probabile,
quam inusitatum, iudices, quam novum, in pane
datum venenum! Faciliusne potuit quam in
poculo? latius potuit abditum aliqua in parte panis
quam si totum colliquefactum in potione esset? 15
celerius potuit comestum quam epotum in venas
atque in omnes partes corporis permanare? facilius
fallere in pane (si esset animadversum) quam in
poculo, cum ita confusum esset ut secerni nullo
modo posset? "At repentina morte periit." Quod 20
si esset ita factum, tamen ea res, propter multorum eiusmodi mortem, satis firmam veneni suspicionem non haberet. Si esset suspiciosum, tamen

ad alios potius quam ad Habitum pertineret.
25 Verum in eo ipso homines impudentissime menti-
untur. Id ut intellegatis, et mortem eius et quemadmodum post mortem in Habitum sit crimen a
matre quaesitum, cognoscite.

29 But Oppianicus was not murdered. Resenting Sassia's
misconduct, he left home and was killed by a fall from his
horse.

Cum vagus et exsul erraret, atque undique exclusus Oppianicus in Falernum se ad L. Quinctium
contulisset, ibi primum in morbum incidit ac satis
vehementer diuque aegrotavit. Cum esset una
5 Sassia, et Sex. Attio quodam, colono, homine
valenti, qui simul esse solebat, familiarius uteretur
quam vir dissolutissimus, incolumi fortuna, pati
posset; Nicostratus quidam, fidelis Oppianici servulus, percuriosus et minime mendax, multa dicitur
10 renuntiare domino solitus esse. Interea Oppianicus
cum iam convalesceret, neque in Falerno impro-
bitatem coloni diutius ferre posset, et huc ad
urbem profectus esset (solebat enim extra portam
aliquid habere conducti), cecidisse ex equo dicitur,
15 et homo infirma valetudine latus offendisse vehementer, et, posteaquam ad urbem cum febri venerit,
paucis diebus esse mortuus. Mortis ratio, iudices,
eiusmodi est, ut aut nihil habeat suspicionis, aut,
si quid habet, id intra parietes in domestico scelere
20 versetur.

PART VI

SASSIA'S LAST ATTEMPT.
INVESTIGATION BY TORTURE

On the death of her husband, Sassia plotted to bring a **30** charge of murder against my client; and held two successive inquiries at which she examined by torture the slave of Oppianicus' doctor, hoping that he would involve Cluentius in his confession.

Post mortem eius Sassia statim moliri nefaria mulier coepit insidias filio: quaestionem habere de viri morte constituit. Emit de A. Rupilio, quo erat usus Oppianicus medico, Stratonem quendam, quasi ut idem faceret, quod Habitus in emendo 5 Diogene fecerat. De hoc Stratone et de Ascla quodam servo suo quaesituram esse dixit. Praeterea servum illum Nicostratum, quem nimium loquacem fuisse, ac nimium domino fidelem arbitrabatur, ab hoc adulescente Oppianico in quaestionem postu- 10 lavit. Hic cum esset illo tempore puer, et illa quaestio de patris sui morte constitui diceretur; etsi illum servum et sibi benevolum esse et patri fuisse arbitrabatur, nihil tamen est ausus recusare. Advocantur amici et hospites Oppianici et ipsius 15 mulieris multi, homines honesti atque omnibus rebus ornati. Tormentis omnibus vehementissimis quaeritur. Cum essent animi servorum et spe et metu tentati, ut aliquid in quaestione dicerent, tamen, ut arbitror, auctoritate advocatorum ad- 20 ducti, in veritate manserunt, neque se quicquam scire dixerunt.

31 She only left off when her cruelty had disgusted the witnesses and without having obtained the evidence she wanted. Strato she restored to high favour!

Quaestio illo die de amicorum sententia dimissa est. Satis longo intervallo post iterum advocantur. Habetur de integro quaestio: nulla vis tormentorum acerrimorum praetermittitur: aversari advocati et iam vix ferre posse: furere crudelis atque importuna mulier, sibi nequaquam, ut sperasset, ea, quae cogitasset, procedere. Cum iam tortor atque essent tormenta ipsa defessa, neque tamen illa finem facere vellet, quidam ex advocatis, homo et honoribus populi ornatus et summa virtute praeditus, intellegere se dixit, non id agi, ut verum inveniretur, sed ut aliquid falsi dicere cogerentur. Hoc postquam ceteri comprobarunt, ex omnium sententia constitutum est, satis videri esse quaesitum. Redditur Oppianico Nicostratus: Larinum ipsa proficiscitur cum suis, maerens, quod iam certe incolumem filium fore putabat, ad quem non modo verum crimen sed ne ficta quidem suspicio perveniret: et cui non modo aperta inimicorum oppugnatio sed ne occultae quidem matris insidiae nocere potuissent. Larinum postquam venit, quae a Stratone illo venenum antea viro suo datum sibi persuasum esse simulasset, instructam ei continuo et ornatam Larini medicinae exercendae causa tabernam dedit.

After three years (during which Sassia established her hold **32**
on the younger Oppianicus by betrothing her daughter to
him) Strato committed burglary and murder at her house.
This gave Sassia the chance for which she had been waiting.

Unum, alterum, tertium annum Sassia quiesce-
bat, ut velle atque optare aliquid calamitatis filio
potius quam id struere et moliri videretur. Tum
interim, Hortensio Q. Metello consulibus, ut hunc
Oppianicum aliud agentem, ac nihil eiusmodi cogi- 5
tantem, ad hanc accusationem detraheret, invito
despondit ei filiam suam, illam, quam ex genero
susceperat, ut eum nuptiis alligatum simul et testa-
menti spe devinctum posset habere in potestate.
Hoc ipso fere tempore Strato ille medicus domi 10
furtum fecit et caedem eiusmodi: cum esset in
aedibus armarium, in quo sciret esse nummorum
aliquantum et auri, noctu duos conservos dor-
mientes occidit in piscinamque deiecit: ipse armarii
fundum exsecuit, et HS** et auri quinque pondo 15
abstulit, uno ex servis, puero non grandi, conscio.
Furto postridie cognito, omnis suspicio in eos
servos, qui non comparebant, commovebatur.
Cum exsectio illa fundi in armario animadverte-
retur, quaerebant homines, quonam modo fieri 20
potuisset. Quidam ex amicis Sassiae recordatus
est, se nuper in auctione quadam vidisse, in rebus
minutis, aduncam ex omni parte dentatam et
tortuosam venire serrulam, qua illud potuisse ita
circumsecari videretur. Ne multa: perquiritur a 25
coactoribus: invenitur ea serrula ad Stratonem
pervenisse. Hoc initio suspicionis orto, et aperte
insimulato Stratone, puer ille conscius pertimuit:

rem omnem dominae indicavit: homines in piscina
30 inventi sunt: Strato in vincula coniectus est: atque
etiam in taberna eius nummi, nequaquam omnes,
reperiuntur.

33 **An inquiry into the burglary was held and the same slaves
once more put to the torture.**

Constituitur quaestio de furto. Nam quid quisquam suspicari aliud potest? An hoc dicitis:
armario expilato, pecunia ablata, non omni re-
cuperata, occisis hominibus, institutam esse quae-
5 stionem de morte Oppianici? cui probatis? quid
est quod minus veri simile proferre potuistis?
Deinde, ut omittam cetera, triennio post mortem
Oppianici de eius morte quaerebatur? Atque etiam
incensa odio pristino, Nicostratum eundem illum
10 tum sine causa in quaestionem postulavit. Oppianicus primo recusavit. Postea, cum illa abduc-
turam se filiam, mutaturam esse testamentum,
minaretur, mulieri crudelissimae servum fidelis-
simum, non in quaestionem tulit, sed plane ad
15 supplicium dedit.

Post triennium igitur agitata denuo quaestio de
viri morte habebatur: et de quibus servis habebatur? Nova, credo, res obiecta, novi quidam
homines in suspicionem vocati sunt. De Stratone
20 et de Nicostrato. Quid? Romae quaesitum de istis
hominibus non erat? Itane tandem? Mulier iam
non morbo, sed scelere furiosa, cum quaestionem
habuisset Romae, cum de T. Annii, L. Rutilii, P.
Saturii, et ceterorum honestissimorum virorum

sententia constitutum esset, satis quaesitum videri; 25
eadem de re triennio post, iisdem de hominibus,
nullo adhibito, non dicam viro (ne colonum forte
adfuisse dicatis) sed bono viro, in filii caput
quaestionem habere conata est?

**The inquiry was supposed to deal with the burglary. Did 34
Strato, then, in confessing to it, let slip some admission
against Cluentius? No; Sassia had not the brains to think
of that. She forged his confession that Cluentius had
poisoned Oppianicus, and forgot to mention the burglary
at all.**

An hoc dicitis: cum haberetur de furto quaestio,
Stratonem aliquid de veneno esse confessum?
Utrum furtum factum non est? At nihil clarius
Larini fuit. An ad Stratonem suspicio non perti-
nuit? At is et ex serrula insimulatus, et a puero 5
conscio est indicatus. An id actum non est in
quaerendo? Quae fuit alia igitur causa quaerendi?
An, id quod dicendum vobis est, et quod tum
Sassia dictitabat, cum de furto quaereretur, tum
Strato iisdem in tormentis dixit de veneno? En 10
hoc illud est, quod ante dixi: mulier abundat audacia: consilio et ratione deficitur. Nam tabellae
quaestionis plures proferuntur, quae recitatae vo-
bisque editae sunt, illae ipsae, quas tum obsignatas
esse dixit: in quibus tabellis de furto littera nulla in- 15
venitur. Non venit in mentem, primum orationem
Stratonis conscribere de furto, post aliquid ad-
iungere dictum de veneno, quod non percontatione
quaesitum sed dolore expressum videretur. Quaestio de furto est, veneni iam suspicione, superiore 20
quaestione, sublata; quod ipsum haec eadem mulier

iudicarat, quae ut Romae de amicorum sententia
statuerat satis esse quaesitum, postea per triennium
maxime ex omnibus servis Stratonem illum dilex-
25 erat, in honore habuerat, commodis omnibus affe-
cerat. Cum igitur de furto quaereretur, et eo furto,
quod ille sine controversia fecerat, tum ille de eo,
quod quaerebatur, verbum nullum fecit? de veneno
statim dixit? de furto, si non eo loco, quo debuit,
30 ne in extrema quidem, aut media, aut in aliqua
denique parte quaestionis, verbum fecit ullum?

35 What an impudent forgery it is! How dare you bring it
into court, Accius, unsigned and unwitnessed? The very
fate of Nicostratus argues the guilty conscience of Sassia.

Iam videtis, illam nefariam mulierem, iudices,
eadem manu, qua, si detur potestas, interficere
filium cupiat, hanc fictam quaestionem con-
scripsisse. Atque istam ipsam quaestionem dicite
5 quis obsignarit. Unum aliquem nominate. Neminem reperietis, nisi forte eiusmodi hominem, quem
ego proferri malim quam neminem nominari. Quid
ais, T. Acci? tu periculum capitis, tu indicium
sceleris, tu fortunas alterius litteris conscriptas in
10 iudicium afferes; neque earum auctorem litterarum,
neque obsignatorem, neque testem ullum nomina-
bis? et, quam tu pestem innocentissimo filio ex
matris sinu deprompseris, hanc hi tales viri com-
probabunt? Esto: in tabellis nihil est auctoritatis.
15 Quid istis hominibus factum est, Stratone et
Nicostrato? Quaero abs te, Oppianice, servo tuo
Nicostrato quid factum esse dicas: quem tu, cum

hunc brevi tempore accusaturus esses, Romam de-
ducere, dare potestatem indicandi, incolumem
denique servare quaestioni, servare his iudicibus, 20
servare huic tempori debuisti. Nam Stratonem
quidem, iudices, in crucem actum esse exsecta
scitote lingua: quod nemo est Larinatium qui
nesciat. Timuit mulier amens non suam conscientiam, non odium municipum, non famam 25
omnium; sed, quasi non omnes eius sceleris testes
essent futuri, sic metuit, ne condemnaretur extrema servuli voce morientis.

What an unnatural monster my client's mother is! She is **36**
the source of all his troubles and is now plotting his death.
She it is who has worked up the whole apparatus of this
trial; and has now come to Rome to enjoy the spectacle of
her son's plight.

Quod hoc portentum, di immortales, quod tantum monstrum in ullis locis? quod tam infestum
scelus et immane, aut unde natum esse dicamus?
Iam enim videtis profecto, iudices, non sine neces-
sariis me ac maximis causis, principio orationis 5
meae de matre dixisse. Nihil est enim mali, nihil
sceleris, quod illa non ab initio filio voluerit, op-
taverit, cogitaverit, effecerit. Nihil est ab Oppianico sine consilio mulieris cogitatum: quod nisi
esset, certe postea, deprehensa re, non illa ut ab 10
improbo viro discessisset, sed ut a crudelissimo
hoste fugisset, domumque illam in perpetuum,
scelere omni affluentem, reliquisset. Non modo id
non fecit, sed ab illo tempore nullum locum prae-
termisit in quo non instrueret insidias aliquas, ac 15

dies omnes ac noctes tota mente mater de pernicie
filii cogitaret. Quae primum ut istum confirmaret
Oppianicum accusatorem filio suo, donis, muneri-
bus, collocatione filiae, spe hereditatis obstrinxit.
20 Neque in eo solum diligens fuit, ut accusatorem
filio suo compararet sed etiam cogitavit, quibus
eum rebus armaret. Hinc enim illae sollicitationes
servorum et minis et promissis: hinc illae infinitae
crudelissimaeque de morte Oppianici quaestiones:
25 quibus finem aliquando non mulieris modus sed
amicorum auctoritas fecit. Ab eodem scelere illae
triennio post habitae Larini quaestiones: eiusdem
amentiae falsae conscriptiones quaestionum: ex
eodem furore etiam illa conscelerata exsectio
30 linguae: totius denique huius ab illa est et inventa
et adornata comparatio criminis. Atque his rebus
cum instructum accusatorem filio suo Romam
misisset, ipsa paullisper, conquirendorum et conducendorum testium causa, Larini est commorata:
35 postea autem, cum appropinquare huius iudicium
ei nuntiatum est, confestim huc advolavit, ne aut
accusatoribus diligentia, aut pecunia testibus de-
esset; aut ne forte mater hoc sibi optatissimum
spectaculum huius sordium atque luctus et tanti
40 squaloris amitteret.

37 What a journey was hers! No one would speak to her or
receive her. The very Gods, whom she dishonours with her
prayers, spurn her from their altars.

Iam vero quod iter Romam eius mulieris fuisse
existimatis? quod ego propter vicinitatem Aqui-

natium et Fabraternorum ex multis audivi et comperi; quos concursus in his oppidis, quantos et virorum et mulierum gemitus esse factos? Mulierem 5 quandam Larino adesse, atque illam usque a mari supero Romam proficisci cum magno comitatu et pecunia, quo facilius circumvenire iudicio capitis atque opprimere filium possit! Nemo erat illorum, paene dicam, quin expiandum illum locum esse 10 arbitraretur, quacunque illa iter fecisset: nemo quin terram ipsam violari, quae mater est omnium, vestigiis consceleratae matris putaret. Itaque nullo in oppido consistendi potestas ei fuit: nemo ex tot hospitibus inventus est, qui non contagionem 15 aspectus fugeret. Nocti se potius ac solitudini quam ulli aut urbi aut hospiti committebat. Nunc vero quid agat, quid moliatur, quid denique quotidie cogitet, quem ignorare nostrum putat? Quos appellarit, quibus pecuniam promiserit, quorum 20 fidem pretio labefactare conata sit, tenemus. Quin etiam nocturna sacrificia, quae putat occultiora esse, sceleratasque eius preces et nefaria vota cognovimus, quibus illa etiam deos immortales de suo scelere testatur, neque intellegit, pietate et re- 25 ligione et iustis precibus deorum mentes, non contaminata superstitione neque ad scelus perficiendum caesis hostiis, posse placari. Cuius ego furorem atque crudelitatem deos immortales a suis aris atque templis aspernatos esse confido.   30

Vos, iudices, quos huic A. Cluentio quasi aliquos deos ad omne vitae tempus fortuna esse voluit, huius importunitatem matris a filii capite depellite. At quae mater? quam caecam crudelitate et scelere
5 ferri videtis: cuius cupiditatem nulla umquam turpitudo retardavit: quae vitiis animi in deterrimas partes iura hominum convertit omnia: cuius ea stultitia est ut eam nemo hominem, ea vis ut nemo feminam, ea crudelitas ut nemo matrem,
10 appellare possit. Atque etiam nomina necessitudinum, non solum naturae nomen et iura mutavit: uxor generi, noverca filii, filiae pelex: eo iam denique adducta est, ut sibi, praeter formam, nihil ad similitudinem hominis reservarit. Quare,
15 iudices, si scelus odistis, prohibete aditum matris a filii sanguine: date parenti hunc incredibilem dolorem ex salute, ex victoria liberum: patimini matrem, ne orbata filio laetetur, victam potius vestra aequitate discedere. Sin autem, id quod
20 vestra natura postulat, pudorem, bonitatem, virtutemque diligitis, levate hunc aliquando supplicem vestrum, iudices, tot annos in falsa invidia periculisque versatum, qui nunc primum post illam flammam, aliorum facto et cupiditate ex-
25 citatam, spe vestrae aequitatis erigere animum, et paullum respirare a metu coepit: cui posita sunt in vobis omnia: quem servatum esse plurimi cupiunt, servare soli vos potestis. Orat vos Habitus, iudices, et flens obsecrat ne se invidiae quae in iudiciis

valere non debet, ne matri cuius vota et preces a 30
vestris mentibus repudiare debetis, ne Oppianico,
homini nefario, condemnato iam et mortuo, condonetis.

If you fail him, he may well regret that the attempt **39**
against his life was not successful. Shew yourselves the
defenders of the innocent, the champions of truth against
prejudice.

Quod si qua calamitas hunc in hoc iudicio afflix-
erit innocentem, ne iste miser, iudices, si, id quod
difficile factu est, in vita remanebit, saepe et
multum queretur, deprehensum esse illud quondam Fabricianum venenum. Quod si tum in- 5
dicatum non esset, non huic aerumnosissimo venenum illud fuisset, sed multorum medicamentum
laborum: postremo etiam fortasse mater exsequias
illius funeris prosecuta, mortem se filii lugere simulasset. Nunc vero quid erit profectum, nisi ut huius 10
ex mediis mortis insidiis vita ad luctum conservata,
mors sepulcro patris privata esse videatur? Satis
diu fuit in miseriis, iudices: satis multos annos ex
invidia laboravit. Nemo huic tam iniquus praeter
parentem fuit, cuius animum non iam expletum 15
esse putemus: vos, qui aequi estis omnibus, qui,
ut quisque crudelissime oppugnatur, eum lenissime
sublevatis, conservate A. Cluentium: restituite incolumem municipio: amicis, vicinis, hospitibus,
quorum studia videtis, reddite: vobis in perpetuum 20
liberisque vestris obstringite. Vestrum est hoc,
iudices, vestrae dignitatis, vestrae clementiae:

recte hoc repetitur a vobis, ut virum optimum
atque innocentissimum, plurimisque mortalibus
25 carum atque iucundissimum, his aliquando cala-
mitatibus liberetis; ut omnes intellegant, in contionibus esse invidiae locum, in iudiciis veritati.

NOTES ON THE TEXT
PART I
Section 1

l. 2. **municipii Larinatis**: Larinas, adjective; Larinum was in Samnium, east of Rome, about 12 miles from the Adriatic. A *municipium* (or county town) had the right of Roman citizenship and was governed by its own laws and magistrates.

l. 5. **Sulla et Pompeio consulibus**, *i.e.* 88 B.C. The Romans dated the year by the names of the consuls for that year.

l. 9. **ut tum habebatur**: note the force of *tum*: his subsequent conduct caused a change of opinion.

inter suos: the reflexive is employed without reference to either the grammatical or the logical subject of the sentence provided that no ambiguity is caused.

honesto et nobili: *not* "honest and noble" but "of high character and rank". It is dangerous to assume that a Latin word bears the same meaning as an English word derived from it.

l. 12. **nefaria libido**: tr. "wicked passion".

l. 14. **in omni causa** = *in tota causa*.

l. 15. **odio et crudelitate**: ablatives of description.

l. 17. **contra quam fas erat**: *contra quam* is here used as a conjunction introducing a comparative clause: "contrary to what was right". *Fas* and *nefas* are what is right and wrong according to divine law.

l. 18. **quoquo modo poterat** = as best she could, somehow or other.

l. 19. **in illa cupiditate**, etc.: tr. "she restrained her feelings".

l. 21. **macula familiae**: objective genitive; tr. "the disgrace she was causing to the family".

l. 24. **consilio ac ratione**: tr. "wisdom and understanding".

l. 25. **illa aetas**: abstract for concrete, "a man of that age".

l. 26. **communi dolore muliebri**: tr. "the resentment which any woman would feel".

l. 27. **angeretur...arbitraretur**: notice the subjunctives, which, with a relative, make the clause adverbial instead of adjectival. Here the sense is causal in *angeretur*, generic ("such as to make her think") in *arbitraretur*.

Section 2

l. 1. **Ecce autem**: notice how Cicero uses these words to startle his audience, introducing a dramatic incident told in short, arresting sentences.

l. 3. **ut...ut**: causal: tr. either "considering..." or "as was natural...".

l. 5. **laetitia...gaudio**: ablatives of cause.

l. 6. **Itaque...noluit**: sarcastic.

l. 8. **nullis auspicibus**, etc.: these are ablatives of attendant circumstances. *Auspicibus* (not *auspiciis*) means some one to take the omens; *auctoribus* means someone to show approval of the wedding, to "give away" the bride.

l. 10. This outburst would not be suited to an English court of law; but Cicero knew that the more excitable Romans would like it.

scelus...libidinem...audaciam: exclamatory accusatives.

praeter hanc unam = *praeter huius unius mulieris scelus*.

l. 11. **in omni vita**: in all (our experience of) life.

l. 13. **nonne timuisse**: the (accusative and) infinitive of indignant exclamation: tr. "to think that...".

l. 18. **familiae, cognationis, nominis**: each expresses a more distant degree of relationship.

Section 3

l. 13. **bello Italico**: the Italian or Social War, 91–88 B.C., in which the Italians secured Roman citizenship.

l. 14. **Asculum**: a town in Picenum, north-east of Rome, where the Social War first broke out.

l. 15. **inter sicarios**: a technical legal term (*quaestio* is understood) for the court that dealt with cases of murder. Here tr. "in the Homicide Court".

l. 21. **illum**: deictic "the younger Oppianicus here"— as prosecutor he would be present in court.

l. 24. **qui nuntiaret**: relative with subjunctive to express purpose.

l. 25. **ager Gallicus**: a strip of land along the Adriatic coast between Ariminum and Ancona, so called because a tribe of Gauls once settled there.

l. 31. **tamen**: "(although all the others had perished) still...".

l. 33. **oppressa morbo**: do not translate this "overcome with disease", but simply "was taken ill". For the circumstances, see § 10.

l. 34. **HS cccc = 400,000** sesterces = rather less than £4000. HS stands for *duo et semis* = 2½ asses = 1 sestertius.

l. 36. **his diebus paucis**: ablative of the time within which: "a few days after this". Compare *brevi tempore* below.

l. 37. **viva Dinaea**: ablative absolute, as also *mortua illa*.

l. 42. **Gallicanum**: an inhabitant of the Ager Gallicus; *vide* note on § 3, l. 25.

l. 44. **tollendum...curavit**: verbs such as *do, trado* and *curo* have the gerundive agreeing with the accusative (their direct object) to express that something is caused to be done.

Section 4

l. 4. **mittunt**: the historic present used for the sake of vividness. This idiom should be avoided in translation. Note that the historic present is followed by the historic sequence.

sibi...esse, etc.: *oratio obliqua*, indirect statement after *litteras mittunt* which is equivalent to a verb of saying.

l. 9. **nomen deferre** (*ad praetorem*) is a technical legal phrase meaning to accuse.

l. 10. **comperisset**: the tense used in *oratio obliqua* for the future perfect in *oratio recta.*

l. 11. **brevi tempore**: see note on *his diebus paucis*, § 3, l. 36.

l. 17. **denuntiarat**: not "who had denounced him"; but "who had given notice (of his intention to prosecute him)".

clamore...ac minis: an instance of the figure of speech, common in Latin, known as hendiadys ("one by two"), *i.e.* one idea is expressed by two nouns joined by a conjunction, instead of by one noun qualified by an adjective. Tr. "with loud threats".

l. 19. **Quintus Metellus**, a general of the senatorial party, took part in the Social War and was of great assistance to Sulla after the latter's return from the East in 83 B.C. He was his colleague in the consulship in 80 B.C.

l. 20. **conscientiae**: consciousness of his guilt, guilty conscience; not to be taken with *sceleris* as a hendiadys.

49

l. 23. per illam L. Sullae vim...: tr. "taking advantage of the victory of violence under Sulla".

l. 25. advolavit: note the metaphor "he swooped down". **quattuorviri:** the council of four, the highest magistrates of a *municipium*; they held office for a year.

l. 29. capitis periculum ostentarat: *periculum* is technically used for the particular danger involved in a trial. Tr. "had threatened him with a capital charge"; but remember that *caput* can mean "civil status" as well as "life". The punishment for a "capital" crime would be exile (loss of civil status) rather than death, which it was illegal to inflict on a Roman citizen, as Oppianicus had cause to be thankful for and Cicero, in the case of Catiline, cause to regret.

l. 30. sequestre: the word is always used by Cicero in connexion with bribery and corruption. It means the go-between, who received the money from the briber and held it till the business for which it was to be given was completed. He then paid it to the persons bribed—unless, like Staienus later on in this story, he kept it to himself!

l. 34. proscriptionis, *i.e.* the placing on a list of the names of people condemned to confiscation of their property and sometimes, as in this case, to death.

l. 36. arbitraretur: subjunctive because *qui* means "of such a kind that".

PART II

Section 5

l. 2. aliquando...aliquamdiu: tr. "at length...for any length of time".

l. 7. qui postulet: causal; *si nubat* "if she should marry him". The apodosis of this remote future condition is *an crudelior illa* (*sit*).

l. 9. humanitas refers to their feelings, **constantia** to their methods. The words are, of course, used ironically.

l. 11. admiratur: expresses not admiration but surprise.

l. 16. domo sibi quaerendum...: "thought he must seek a remedy from (*not* in) his own home to (remove) the (cause of) delay", *i.e.* the remedy was not far to seek—as is explained by what follows.

50

l. 20. **Teanum** in Apulia, so distinguished from Teanum Sidicinum in Campania. *Teani* is locative.

l. 22. **ludis...diebus**: ablatives of time when.

l. 24. **mali**: partitive genitive, as commonly after *nihil*, *aliquid*—cf. French *rien de, quelque chose de.*

l. 26. **hora undecima**: the period between sunrise and sunset was divided into twelve equal hours, as also the period between sunset and sunrise. These hours, of course, varied in length according to the time of year.

l. 27. **antequam luceret**: note the subjunctive, which conveys (literally) an idea of purpose—Oppianicus' purpose to destroy the corpse before there was light enough for people to see it.

l. 29. **quisquam** is used because the sentence is virtually negative.

l. 31. **sibi**: many verbs of taking away are used with the dative (especially of a person), instead of the ablative, of separation.

l. 34. **Dies nondum...cum...necatur**: a case of the inverted use of *cum*, *i.e.* the *cum* clause contains what is really the principal sentence. It is followed by the indicative.

l. 36. **laetanti...confirmato**: not dative but ablative absolute. The reference is to Sassia.

l. 39. **quod**: "whereas", commonly so used to contrast opposites. Here the verbal contrast is rather forced. The idea seems to be that while love of their children makes most people more anxious for money (*cupidiores*) than they are by nature, love of money made Oppianicus find it pleasanter (*iucundius*) to murder his children than he would have even by *his* nature.

Section 6

l. 1. **Sentio, iudices...**: a fine rhetorical passage in which Cicero drives home his conclusion, the guilt of Oppianicus, before proceeding to the next part of his story. Note how the effect is heightened by every device of form— the arrangement of the sentences, their vigour and balance, the repetition of vital words—the whole culminating in the final *innocentem.*

pro...humanitate: *pro* = by reason of, considering,

51

Humanitas means those feelings which every (decent) human being has.

l. 3. **tandem:** tr. "indeed" or "I ask you". Cf. *Quousque tandem abutere, o Catilina, patientia nostra?*

l. 4. **illos...vos:** this contrast, which runs through the whole passage, is between the jury under Junius before whom Oppianicus had been prosecuted by Cluentius eight years before and the present jury before whom Ciuentius was being prosecuted by the younger Oppianicus.

quibus: dative of the agent with the gerundive.

l. 13. **praesentis:** not "present" but "face to face".

l. 15. **oderant:** impartiality was not, apparently, expected of a Roman jury!

l. 20. **diceretur:** we might have expected the indicative (the clause being purely temporal) to correspond with *cum a me dicuntur* above. This is an example of the Latin tendency to put any past tense in the subjunctive after *cum*, though retaining the indicative for a present tense.

l. 22. **innocentem:** note the sarcastic emphasis which is put on this word by its position.

Section 7

l. 2. **causae:** dative after *propiora*; *huius* is masculine.

l. 3. **Vos...teneatis:** *vos* is subject of *teneatis*. The subjunctive is jussive, partly dependent on *quaeso*.

l. 6. **uti:** governed by *mihi esse propositum* supplied from the previous sentence.

l. 13. **ad:** "in addition to".

l. 17. **Eodem:** it was *not* the same poison, but the same method, namely, poison. Tr. "he used poison, again, when he murdered...".

l. 18. **ipso fraterno parricidio:** "the murder of a brother by itself", apart from anything else. *Parricidium* (which is probably not derived from *pater* or *parens*) is used for the murder of anybody.

l. 20. **aditum...munivit:** a metaphor from road-making. Tr. "paved the way". Roman roads were for military purposes and were meant to last.

Section 8

l. 1. **Quid?** Marks Cicero's transition to another point. Tr. "Again".

l. 2. **recenti re**: probably ablative absolute, *recens* having the form, and here the construction, of a participle.

l. 4. **perdita...egestate**: these are ablatives of description, whereas *arte* is governed by *praeditus*.

l. 6. **qui...blanditiis**, etc.: tr. "by flattery and obsequious attentions, he succeeded in worming his way into the confidence of Asuvius".

l. 9. **tamquam aliqua**: both words are introduced, like *quasi aliquos* in § 38, l. 1, to change a bold metaphor into a simile, which the literally-minded Romans preferred. The idea is that of taking a town by storm and is continued in *capere* and *expugnare*.

l. 14. **posse arbitrati sunt**: *se* is often omitted after verbs of perceiving and declaring.

l. 15. **vestigiis**: the ablative used to express "the road by which".

l. 18. **conscio...conviva...adiutore**: "known...shared ...abetted by...".

l. 19. **longum est mihi dicere**: "it *would be* tedious to tell". The indicative is here used in the apodosis of a (virtual) conditional sentence instead of the subjunctive, as commonly with verbs expressing duty, probability, etc.

l. 25. **obsignatores**: witnesses who set their seals to a will.

l. 27. **nossent**: note the force of the subjunctive.

l. 29. **brevi...tempore**: see note on *his diebus paucis*, § 3, l. 36.

l. 30. **hortulos**: both *hortus* and *hortulus* have, in the plural only, the meaning of a park or pleasure gardens; here tr. "the Gardens".

Section 9

l. 1. **unum...et alterum diem**: "for one day and a second", *i.e.* for one or two days.

desideraretur: just as an action extending over some time up to and including the present is expressed in Latin by a present and not by a perfect tense (*e.g. iampridem cupio* = I have long been wishing); so an action which has similarly extended up to, and so as to include, a point in past time is expressed by an imperfect and not by a pluperfect.

l. 2. **ubi ex consuetudine quaerebatur**: tr. "where his habits led people to look for him".

l. **9. triumvir**: *i.e.* one of the three *III viri capitales*, or subordinate police-magistrates.

l. **19. ex petulanti...scurra**: tr. "from being a brazen and worthless parasite". The word *scurra*, from having the purely complimentary sense of an elegant and witty man-about-town, came to be used of a professional wit employed to be amusing at the dinner table.

l. **20. discordiis civitatis**: *i.e.* the struggle between Marius and Sulla.

l. **21. eam columnam**: *i.e.* the Columna Maenia which stood at the south end of the Forum. Here the *III viri capitales* held their court to try the lowest class of offenders.

l. **22. conviciis**: ablative of attendant circumstances, **suffragiis** ablative of the instrument.

l. **23. rem...transigit**: tr. "he came to terms".

l. **27. in quo**: *sc. iudicio.* Tr. "by which it was made clear that the person primarily implicated was Oppianicus".

Section 10

l. **4. victorem**: tr. "successful".

l. **5. curari...curante**: tr. "she absolutely declined to be attended by one whose attentions had lost her all her children". *Suos omnes* hardly seems to square with the account given in § 3.

l. **7. pharmacopolam circumforaneum**: tr. "a travelling quack".

l. **9. duobus milibus HS**: less than £20.

l. **11. properaret...restarent**: the subjunctives express his excuses and almost quote his words: "I am in a hurry: I have many country towns to visit".

l. **14. punctum**: accusative of "time how long".
temporis: partitive genitive.

l. **16. fuisset**: subjunctive, because it explains how it was that Oppianicus was able to get hold of the will; pluperfect, because Dinaea's daughter Magia was now dead.
digito: the will was on waxed tablets and so could be rubbed out.

l. **23. tabulas...censorias**: the public records kept at each *municipium* by its own censors.

l. **24. decuriones**: the town council.
universi: unanimous.

Section 11

l. 1. rationem...rem: "financial dealings...business dealings".

l. 3. tutorem: under Roman law a woman or a minor could only transact business through a trustee.

l. 6. abhorrebant does not, like *aspernabantur* and *fugiebant*, take an accusative; we must understand *ab eo*.

l. 13. nihil: we should make it personal and say "no one".

l. 15. instituta ratione vitae: tr. "his settled plan of life".

l. 17. iuste: consistently with justice.

pie: consistently with the claims of relationship.

l. 18. quoquo modo...illo modo: it is easy to see what this means but difficult to translate it. To say "he preferred to prosecute as best he could rather than to die as otherwise he would" preserves the form of the Latin—but sounds silly.

PART III

Section 12

l. 11. bona eius omnia: what had happened to Cluentius' sister, Cluentia? for if he had died without making a will she would have been entitled to a share of the property. We must suppose that she had died or married again.

l. 12. aucta...orbata: both participles are nominative.

Section 13

l. 2. Aletrium: a country town some 50 miles east-south-east of Rome.

l. 5. prope aequabilis: "generally consistent".

l. 10. ita viverent ut: "lived on the assumption that...".

l. 13. circumscriptiones: frauds on minors were specially punishable under Roman law.

l. 21. Cleophantus: a Greek name; the Romans did not think medicine a profession for a gentleman!

l. 24. frugi: an indeclinable adjective, originally the dative of *frux* and so meaning profitable; hence, of a slave who looked after his master's property well, thrifty, honest or virtuous.

l. 32. Ne multis: a good example of ellipsis, *i.e.* the omission of words which can easily be supplied from the context. Tr. "in short".

l. 35. obsignata: the money was in a sealed packet.

dabatur: the tense marks that it was in the act of being handed over. Scamander was caught red-handed.

l. 37. Pro di immortales: *pro* is not a preposition but an interjection.

Section 14

l. 3. ita...citatum esse...ut: a restrictive use of *ut* common in Cicero, the translation of which must depend on the context. Here tr. "he was put on his trial in such circumstances that...".

l. 4. semel atque iterum: *i.e.* the previous convictions of Scamander and Fabricius.

l. 6. nomen...detulit: *i.e. ad praetorem.* See note § 4 (l. 9) on *nomen deferre.*

l. 8. Integrum consilium: "the jury was unbiased" (by bribery); the same idea is repeated in the next clause.

l. 11. Itum est in consilium: "the jury considered their verdict". Note the difference in the meaning of *consilium* here and in the previous sentence.

l. 13. prima actione: in recording his verdict a Roman juror might mark his tablet either "A." (*absolvo*, "not guilty") or "C." (*condemno*, "guilty") or "N.L." (*non liquet*, "not proven"). The verdict was decided by a majority. If the majority voted "N.L.", the case was heard again (*secunda actio*) and so on until a majority for "A." or "C." was obtained. It is important to remember this procedure when reading § 22 below.

l. 17. daretur: final subjunctive.

Section 15

l. 6. consilia conscientiasque: abstract for concrete. Tr. "abettors and accessories".

l. 13. eo animo ut...: tr. "inclined to...".

l. 14. in honore...ponerent: a metaphor from keeping accounts, to put down on the right side; here tr. "to consider as an honour".

l. 16. Citatur reus: notice how Cicero keeps up the interest of his hearers by a change of style, passing from the "periodic" style to short, staccato sentences without connecting words.

l. 17. re iudicata: the verdicts given against Scamander and Fabricius would not be evidence against Oppianicus in English law.

alte petito: tr. "far fetched".

l. 26. praevaricari: originally used of a ploughman who drives a crooked furrow; hence of a man who "does not go straight". Here of a barrister who acts in collusion with the other side, pretending to speak in the interests of his client, but actually doing so in the interests of the other side.

l. 29. ex intimo artificio: tr. "from the secrets of his stock-in-trade".

Respicite: it seems impossible to reproduce Cicero's joke in English. The word *respicere* has two meanings in Latin, "to look behind one" and "to respect". Caepasius of course used it in the latter sense, while Cicero uses *respexit* (l. 5) in the former sense.

l. 34. ridere, etc.: historic infinitives common in vivid passages.

l. 35. eripi, etc.: accusative and infinitive governed by the previous historic infinitives.

l. 36. loco: a purple patch or stock passage.

l. 39. reliqua...perorare: to finish his peroration, his concluding passage.

Section 16

l. 11. quod...voluisset: the alleged reason, therefore in the subjunctive.

l. 13. consequebatur: note the force of the imperfect, "was trying to gain".

l. 20. rerum iudicatarum: judicial decisions, verdicts.

l. 21. libidinem: caprice.

PART IV
Section 17

l. 4. necesse (*est*) may be followed either by the accusative and infinitive, or by the dative and infinitive or by the subjunctive.

l. 16. Statium Albium refers to the elder Oppianicus; Oppianice in the next sentence to the younger, his son; and ab Oppianico, in the sentence after, again refers to the father.

l. 18. Titus Accius, to whom Cicero patronizingly

refers elsewhere as a "worthy and fluent young man", was the counsel briefed by the younger Oppianicus for the prosecution of Cluentius.

eloquentia...pietate: "the eloquence of an advocate... the mute loyalty of a son". *Pietas* expresses a man's duty to his father, children, relatives, country, etc.

l. 21. negate...in eo loco: "stand up in your place and deny it".

l. 23. quod abstulistis: for the recovery of the money from Staienus, see § 23.

Section 18

l. 1. Repetam paullo altius bears a different meaning from that of *alte petito* in § 15. Here it means "I will go back a little".

l. 4. Vos, quaeso: *vos* is nominative.

l. 6. conventu...auribus: the two pairs of words each form a hendiadys and should be translated in each case by an adjective and noun: "hushed assembly...sympathetic hearing".

l. 9. ex eo quod: "from the fact that...".

l. 15. ut eo fautore...: tr. "so that he found in him a more zealous partisan". A juror was not supposed to be biased on either side.

l. 18. ne sua quidem sententia: Fabricius had "voted against himself" by bolting from the court, as described in § 15.

l. 19. remediis: ablative of the instrument.

l. 23. aliqua ex parte: "to a certain extent".

l. 25. capiti ac fortunis: a regular formula to express a man's social and political rights.

l. 29. possit: after *negavit* we should have expected *posset*. The present tense is retained from the *oratio recta* for the sake of vividness.

l. 31. cum hominibus nobilissimis: *i.e.* (in competition) with them.

invidiam atque offensionem: the "misfortune" would be the consequence of the unpopularity.

l. 34. HS sescenta quadraginta milia: 640,000 sesterces, about £6000.

l. 38. rationibus: literally "accounts". Tr. "nothing would suit his book better".

Section 19

l. 2. domi, being a locative, can properly have a prepositional phrase with *in* in apposition to it.

l. 10. Praecipitantem: notice the alliteration which helps to convey the sense of "pushing him over".

l. 12. ut pecuniam...polliceatur explains what the *consilium* was.

l. 16. destitutione iratos Oppianico: *destitutione* is ablative of the cause, *Oppianico* dative after *iratos*.

l. 17. praeposterus means one who puts the cart before the horse; **perversus** means crooked in character. Tr. "in his usual muddling way". The somewhat elaborate jest which follows is difficult to explain and impossible to translate. It turns on the literal meanings of the jurors' names, *i.e.* Bulbus means an onion which was eaten as the savoury at the end of the Roman meal (not at the beginning; hence Staienus is *praeposterus*); and Gutta means a drop, suggesting a drop of sweet salad oil such as might be sprinkled on the onion. This culinary metaphor is carried further in the word *conditor* which, according as the "i" is long or short, comes either from *condio*, "to season" or "spice", or from *condo*, "to found"; the phrase finds a sort of parallel in our "head cook and bottle-washer". This whole passage may be a little cheap, but it may well have sounded very funny to the jury.

l. 19. quaesierat: *quaero* has here its meaning of "to gain", cf. *quaestus*. Bulbus had "made nothing" for some time and was yawning with hunger and boredom.

l. 20. Quid tu (*ais*)? In our idiom, "I say".

l. 21. ne gratis...: a roundabout way of saying "so that we may make something out of our services to the State".

l. 23. quadraginta milia: rather more than £350.

l. 26. conditor: for this and the subsequent puns see note on *praeposterus* above.

Section 20

l. 1. cum...videbatur: the indicative as usual with "inverted" *cum*.

l. 2. confirmator: a man who would guarantee that the sequester, with whom the money had been deposited, would pay up.

l. 5. **ex imaginibus Aeliorum**: in the *atrium* (hall) of a Roman noble's house were hung the *imagines* (portrait-masks) of his ancestors. The *ius imaginum* (right to display these) was enjoyed only by those families whose ancestors had held the higher public offices. One such family was that of the Aelii; and Staienus, wishing to pass himself off as a member of it, had to decide on a cognomen to show to which branch (*familia*) of the family (*gens*) he claimed to belong. The gens Aelia had several branches, with cognomina such as Ligur, Paetus, etc.: but Staienus was wise enough to choose the name Paetus and not Ligur; otherwise people might have thought that "he took his name from his race and not his family"—the point being that the Ligurians were a boorish tribe, dusky in complexion and notoriously treacherous!

l. 12. **incubaret**: "was brooding over"; subjunctive because of its concessive force.

l. 17. **pulchre asseverat**: "blandly asserted".

Section 21

l. 1. **Manarat...**: "had leaked out in court".

l. 5. **Canutius**: already mentioned in § 6 as Cluentius' counsel at the trial of Oppianicus.

l. 6. **qui quodam odore...sensisset**: causal subjunctive. Tr. "who had somehow got wind of...".

l. 7. **neque dum** = *et nondum*.

l. 8. **pronuntiari: Dixerunt**: when both sides had stated their case, the herald of the court (*praeco*) announced "Dixerunt" (the pleadings are finished), as a signal for the jury to consider their verdict. *Pronuntiari* is impersonal. Canutius, by waiving his right of reply and thus springing the pronouncement on the jury, hoped to upset his opponents' plans should the bribery not have been completed.

l. 12. **absolutio**: if the voting resulted in a tie, the accused was given the benefit of the doubt and acquitted.

l. 13. **nummum**: the genitive plural in -*um* of the second declension is common with nouns denoting coins, weights and measures, etc.

l. 14. **ad cumulum**: to top the heap, crown the total.

l. 16. **Atque etiam** resumes the direct narrative after a digression dealing with Oppianicus' calculations.

l. 18. **apud iudicem**: "before an arbitrator" appointed by the praetor in a civil suit. One can hardly understand the laxity which would allow a juror to be absent from court when the case was actually being heard!

l. 23. **ut ne**: used for *ne* with no difference of meaning.

Aelio: Quinctius thought it more impressive to deck Staienus in his borrowed plumes.

l. 24. **viatores**: officials in the service of a tribune.

neglegentius: an "absolute" comparative, "somewhat slackly".

l. 27. **pro potestate**: as tribune, Quinctius had the right of prohibition, different from, and not so formidable as, *intercessio*.

Section 22

l. 2. **quae tum erat potestas**: at the time of the trial of Oppianicus, 74 B.C., the *lex Cornelia* of Sulla was in operation, by which the accused had the right to choose whether the jurors should record their votes openly or by secret ballot: previously they had voted by ballot only. The word *tum* shows that this law was no longer in operation at the time of the trial of Cluentius, 66 B.C.

l. 5. **omnes**: probably refers not to the jurors as a whole but to the venal jurors.

campo: *sc. Martio*, where the elections (*comitia*) were held.

l. 12. **Ecce tibi**: *tibi* is "ethic" dative. Tr. "lo and behold!"

l. 18. **ex vetere...iudiciorum**: literally means "from that old training in trials"; it may be translated "jurors of the old school".

l. 21. **pecunia oppugnatum**: explains their suspicions, *i.e.* "that he was the victim of bribery", and is the matter referred to by *re*.

l. 22. **primo** = *prima actione*, on which *vide* note on § 14, l. 13.

l. 24. **quo quisque...fecerit**: the indirect question is in apposition to *hoc*. The thoughts of the "severi homines" were something as follows: "motive is the important thing to consider. Staienus and Co. are venal: their motive is therefore bad. They voted 'guilty', so we ought to vote 'not guilty'. But despite that, we cannot stultify our own verdicts on Scamander and Fabricius".

l. 31. **ambitio**: properly means the giving of bribes at an election. Here it means corruption in general.

Section 23

l. 4. ut...egerit de pecunia: "how he raised the question of the money".

Section 24

l. 3. primum...deinde...postremo: note the regular sequence for expressing "in the first place...the second place...the third place (or lastly)".

l. 5. condemnatum: *i.e.* by the verdicts passed on his agents.

l. 6. pecunia: ablative.

l. 10. Fabriciis: Fabricius and his freedman, Scamander, are meant.

Section 25

l. 2. profectio pecuniae = *unde profecta sit pecunia.*

l. 3. Confecit tabulas: "kept his accounts". It is to this account keeping that *haec res* refers in the next sentence.

l. 7. causa...meditatione: in English we should make *meditatio* the subject. In Latin a concrete subject is preferred to an abstract.

l. 11. vestigiis...odoranda...cubile: these are all hunting metaphors, and refer to the trail, the scent and the lair of a wild animal.

l. 13. HS IↃCXL: HS stands for sesterces, see note on § 3, l. 34. IↃ = D = 500; so that IↃCXL = 640. The line over the numerals signifies "a thousand times"; so that the whole sum of HS IↃCXL = 640,000 sesterces or nearly £6000.

l. 15. At enim: constantly used to introduce an imaginary objection; "but, you will say".

l. 18. cum iretur...cum mittebant: strictly speaking, when *cum* introduces a clause which is purely temporal, the verb, whatever its tense, should be in the indicative. However, with past tenses, even in a purely temporal clause, the subjunctive came to be preferred. In this case one can only suppose that the purely temporal nature of the clause was more in Cicero's mind when he said *mittebant* than when he said *iretur*, *e.g.* "when the jury were going...at the moment when they were closing the proceedings".

l. 24. obsidem: here = a pledge or guarantee.

l. 33. gratiae conciliandae: apparently Accius had put forward the defence that the 640,000 sesterces were given to Staienus, not as a means to bribe the jury, but just as a present, "to effect a reconciliation" with him!

l. 37. Archimedes: the famous mathematician who lived at Syracuse in the third century B.C. and whose tomb was discovered by Cicero when he was quaestor there in 75 B.C.

Quare...: notice the elaborate rhetorical arrangement of this passage.

l. 43. eo: thither, *i.e.* to Oppianicus.

l. 44. invidiam: the "prejudice" worked up against Cluentius after the trial among people who were persuaded that Oppianicus had been "the innocent victim of corruption".

PART V

Section 26

l. 2. Veneficii crimen...paratum: answers the question asked in the last sentence, *venenum paratum* being in apposition to *crimen* and explaining what the charge was.

huic: deictic, "here in court".

l. 10. in se admisit: literally, "admitted against himself"; *i.e.* had on his conscience.

l. 13. ille verbum...nullum potuerit: he had apparently left all the "eloquentia" to Accius and had discreetly maintained an attitude of what Cicero calls in § 17 "tacita pietas". There was nothing to be feared from him, and Sassia could always have found another accuser if necessary.

l. 15. An ut...decederet: gives a second (ironical) answer to the question "what was Cluentius' motive?" The clause being "final", we should have expected *sua* instead of *eius*; but the main sentence (to be supplied from the context) is only vaguely present in the speaker's mind. *Ut nihil* occurs, instead of the *ne quidquam* to be expected in a final clause, in order to preserve the balance between this clause and the next.

l. 19. quae deinde: "what is the meaning of...?"

l. 21. non committam: literally, "I will not bring it about that I shall seem...". Tr. "I will not give grounds for suspecting that...".

l. 27. crudior: *crudus* literally means "raw". Here the

comparative (which is "absolute") means "suffering somewhat from indigestion".

ut aetas illa fert: abstract for concrete. Tr. "as young
men will".

l. 32. ex illo loco: *i.e.* from the other side, the accuser's.

l. 34. Quod recita: addressed to the clerk of the court
who, when Cicero had finished his next sentence, read out
the father's deposition.

Tu autem: addressed to the father of Balbutius.

l. 38. ut ne: see note § 21 (l. 23) on these words.

Section 27

This volume contains no finer specimen of Cicero's
eloquence than the latter part of this section.

l. 6. conflatum: the metaphor is taken from the act of
blowing up a fire.

l. 19. exsulis testimonio: apart from being unable to
enter Rome, Oppianicus had lost his civic rights and could
not therefore take part in any legal proceeding.

l. 23. damnati and the other genitives explain *illam*:
"such a life, the life of...".

l. 29. quod: by attraction into the gender and number
of the predicate, *perfugium*.

l. 30. animi et virtutis: hendiadys for "any spirit (or,
as we should say, spark) of manliness". Suicide was not
looked upon as wrong until Christian times.

l. 38. reliquisse: by attraction to *offendisse*, instead of
the subjunctive.

l. 39. uxorum: a pardonable exaggeration. As far as
we know he only murdered his first wife, Cluentia.

l. 41. quod omnes intellegunt: it is interesting to see
that no intelligent person was expected to believe in the
traditional Hades. Cicero had, however, a firm belief in
personal immortality.

Section 28

l. 2. Quid huic: "what connexion had he?"

atque adeo: "and what is more".

l. 6. potissimum: an adverb, to be taken closely with
ei: "especially to one whom...". *Illius* refers, of course, to
Oppianicus.

l. 9. Habiti exemplo: *i.e.* in putting the agent on trial
before the principal.

l. 17. facilius fallere: *sc. potuit.*

l. 21. ea res: *i.e. repentina mors.*

l. 25. in eo ipso: the whole story of Oppianicus' death.

Section 29

l. 1. undique exclusus: tr. "finding all doors shut against him".

l. 2. in Falernum: *sc. agrum.* The famous wine-growing district, in northern Campania.

l. 4. una is an adverb.

l. 5. homine valenti: "a lusty fellow".

l. 7. incolumi fortuna: ablative absolute equivalent to a conditional. She was on more intimate terms with him than even a dissolute husband could have endured if his fortunes had remained unimpaired.

l. 8. posset is imperfect subjunctive because it expresses the same time as *uteretur.*

servulus: the diminutive in Latin may give either a contemptuous or as here a good-humoured turn to the word. Tr. "a favourite slave".

l. 12. ad urbem: *ad =* to the neighbourhood of. As an exile he was debarred from entering the city.

l. 14. aliquid...conducti: a contemptuous phrase: "some hired lodging". See note on § 5, l. 24.

l. 15. homo infirma valetudine: explains why the injury to his side became so serious. Tr. "sick man as he was".

l. 17. Mortis ratio: tr. "the circumstances of his death".

l. 19. in domestico scelere: is this a hint at Sassia?

PART VI

Section 30

l. 5. quod Habitus...fecerat: for the purchase of Diogenes, see § 13.

l. 7. quaesituram esse dixit, cf. § 8 (l. 14), *posse arbitrati sunt* and note.

l. 10. in quaestionem: in Rome, as in Greece, a slave was not allowed to give evidence except under torture. The presumption was that he would not otherwise speak the truth!

l. 16. homines honesti: it is surprising to hear, after

§11, that Oppianicus had any friends who could be so described!

l. 20. auctoritate: the moral support of these honourable men.

Section 31

l. 4. aversari...posse...furere: historic infinitives. See note on § **15** (l. **34**), *ridere*. **procedere** is accusative and infinitive, object of *furere*.

l. 11. non id agi: "that the object of the inquiry was, not...".

l. 14. videri: their actual words were: "It seems to us that the inquiry has gone far enough".

l. 17. non modo...ne...quidem: strictly speaking there should be a second *non* after the *modo*; but it is frequently omitted in sentences of this type.

l. 23. simulasset: subjunctive because the sense is concessive.

instructam...et ornatam: tr. "furnished and stocked".

Section 32

l. 3. videretur: consecutive subjunctive.

l. 4. Hortensio, Q. Metello consulibus: *i.e.* 69 B.C.

l. 5. aliud agentem: lit. "doing something else", and so, with his mind or his interests elsewhere: conversely, *hoc agere* = to attend.

l. 7. filiam suam: Auria, her daughter by Aulus Aurius Melinus whom she had enticed away from her own daughter Cluentia, see § 1.

l. 12. sciret: the subjunctive is probably due to a looseness of expression by which the verb of "knowing" is put into the subjunctive instead of the thing known: *i.e.* we might expect *in quo esset* (subjunctive as being part of his thought) or *in quo esse sciebat*.

nummorum...auri: coined money and (uncoined) gold.

l. 15. HS:** the figures giving the actual sum are missing from the MSS.

auri quinque pondo: in this expression *libras* came to be omitted and *pondo* to be treated as an indeclinable noun. The literal meaning is "five (pounds) of gold by weight".

l. 22. in rebus minutis: "among the odds and ends".

l. 23. aduncam...serrulam: a curious instrument and therefore more easily recognizable and useful as evidence.

66

It sounds like a sort of brace-and-bit, *tortuosam* describing the crooked handle of the brace, and the rest of the description applying to the bit, which is small (*serrula*) with teeth (*dentatam*) all round (*ex omni parte*) the edge, which curve away from one another (*aduncam*). "A small curved saw with crooked teeth all round" may serve as a translation.

l. 26. coactoribus: agents employed by an auctioneer to go round after a sale and collect the money from purchasers.

Section 33

l. 2. An hoc dicitis: introduces the second of two alternatives, the first being contained in the preceding question.

l. 8. Atque etiam...: the sense demands that we supply from the context some such phrase as: "yes, his death *was* the object of the inquiry", and then follows *atque etiam*: "and what is more", etc.

l. 14. ad supplicium should not be translated "for torture", which, for a slave, is implied by the words *in quaestionem*. Tr. "not for examination but simply for execution".

l. 19. De Stratone, etc.: *sc. quaestio est habita.*

l. 21. Itane tandem? "is it possible?"

l. 22. morbo: disease of the mind, madness.

l. 26. triennio post: *triennio* is in the ablative, *post* is an adverb. *Post* is used as a preposition in the phrase *post triennium*.

l. 27. colonum: *i.e.* Sextus Attius, *vide* § 29.

Section 34

l. 11. quod ante dixi: Cicero refers to a similar remark which he had made earlier in a part of his speech which has not been included in this volume.

l. 12. consilio et ratione: "judgment and common sense".

tabellae quaestionis: memoranda of the confessions said to have been made at the inquiry.

l. 14. obsignatas: *i.e. ab advocatis.* Cf. § 8 (l. 25), note on *obsignatores*.

l. 20. superiore quaestione: ablative of the instrument.

l. 22. iudicarat: *i.e.* by loading Strato with favours.

quae is therefore almost causal, "in as much as she...", "for she...".

Section 35

l. 6. **eiusmodi hominem**: Sextus Attius again.

l. 9. **fortunas...conscriptas**: literally, "the fortunes of another put down in writing"; we might say, "a document involving the fortunes of another".

l. 12. **filio**: dative of disadvantage.

l. 14. **Esto**: contemptuous, "enough!"

l. 15. **hominibus**: the ablative with *facere* ("to do something with somebody") is instrumental.

l. 21. **Nam**: introduces Cicero's reason for having asked this awkward question.

l. 23. **scitote**: notice the impressive form. Tr. "I have to inform you, gentlemen, that his tongue was cut out and he was then crucified".

l. 27. **sic metuit, ne**: "her one fear was".

l. 28. **servuli**: *vide* note on this word, § 29 (l. 8). Here the force of the diminutive combines pity for Strato and contempt for Sassia. Tr. "a poor dying slave".

Section 36

This section and the next bring the speech to its culmination in a tremendous indictment of Sassia, gathering up and emphasizing the charges brought against her in the first two sections of this volume.

l. 3. **scelus**: abstract for concrete. It can be effectively retained in translation.

l. 7. **voluerit...**: note the crescendo of these verbs, each of which is stronger than the last.

l. 16. **mater**: throughout this indictment Cicero omits no artifice which may heighten the contrast between Sassia's relationship to Cluentius and her behaviour towards him.

l. 33. **conducendorum**: she had to hire them!

l. 36. **advolavit**: *vide* note on the same word, § 4 (l. 25).

l. 39. **sordium...squaloris**: this is no metaphorical reference to Cluentius' unhappy plight, but refers literally to the "squalid mourning and unkempt attire" which the defendant in a serious case usually wore to excite the compassion of the jury!

68

Section 87

l. 2. **propter vicinitatem**: because these towns were near Arpinum where Cicero was born.

l. 4. **quos concursus...esse factos** resumes the sentence interrupted by the parenthesis *quod..comperi*, and is the object of *existimatis*.

l. 5. **Mulierem...adesse** expresses what people said or thought as they groaned: "To think that a woman...is here and has started to go all the way...!"

l. 6. **mare superum**: *i.e.* the Adriatic.

l. 14. **consistendi potestas**: permission to break her journey.

l. 15. **hospitibus** = inn-keepers.

contagionem aspectus: if not actually "evil eye", tr. "her baleful glance".

l. 19. **nostrum**: partitive genitive. The form *nostri* is objective.

l. 22. **occultiora**: "absolute" comparative. Tr. "so secret".

l. 24. **quibus**: ablative of the instrument.

Section 88

l. 1. **quasi...deos** is a simile: for *quasi* changing a metaphor into a simile, see note on *tamquam aliqua*, § 8 (l. 9).

l. 5. **turpitudo**: here = (sense of) shame.

l. 6. **quae vitiis...convertit omnia**: tr. "whose vicious nature has utterly degraded every institution of mankind".

l. 8. **eam...hominem**: a good reminder that *homo* means a human being.

l. 10. **nomina necessitudinum**: the names we give to relationships.

l. 12. **uxor generi**, etc.: in *Orator*, § 107, Cicero recalls with satisfaction this specimen of his power of invective. **pelex** may be translated "rival".

l. 13. **nihil ad similitudinem**: nothing which makes for, is in the direction of....

l. 17. **liberum**: the plural makes the sense general; tr. "of a son".

l. 18. **filio**: ablative of separation, with *orbata*.

l. 21. **levate...aliquando**: "raise up at last".

l. 24. **flammam**, *i.e. invidiae*.

l. 26. cui: dative of advantage.

l. 32. condonetis: *condonare* = literally "to make a present of": here tr. "to sacrifice".

Section 89

l. 6. venenum is the predicate, illud the subject: this becomes clear at once if the sentence is read aloud.

l. 8. exsequias...funeris: "his funeral procession".

l. 10. Nunc vero: "But as it is".

l. 12. sepulcro patris: see note on *filio*, § 38 (l. 18).

l. 15. cuius animum non...putemus: *cuius* has the force of *ut eius* followed by a consecutive subjunctive, its antecedent being *Nemo*. Tr. "No one has been so unfair to my client...that we may not suppose his resentment to be now fully satisfied". *Iniquus* prepares us for the contrast with *aequi* in the next sentence.

l. 17. ut quisque crudelissime...eum, etc.: tr. "grant your gentlest succour to those most cruelly assailed".

l. 18. incolumem: *i.e.* with his rights as a citizen unimpaired.

l. 21. obstringite: literally, "tie him to"; tr. "make him a debtor to...".

l. 26. contionibus: the sort of public meeting at which Quinctius succeeded in working up all the prejudice against Cluentius.

VOCABULARY

ABBREVIATIONS

A., abbrev. for **Aulus**

ā, ab, abs, prep. *by* (a person), *from, on the side of*

abdo, 3, abdidi, abditum, *conceal*

abhorreo, 2, *shrink from, refuse*

absolūtio, -ōnis, f. *acquittal*

absolvo, 3, absolvi, absolūtum, *acquit*

absum (sum), *am distant from*

abundo, 1, *am full of*

āc, conj. see **atque**

accēdo, 3, accessi, accessum, *approach, enter upon, am added, attach itself*

accessio, -ōnis, f. *addition*

accipio (capio), *accept, take*

accommodātus, adj. *well-suited, practised*

accūsātio, -ōnis, f. *prosecution*

accūsātor, -ōris, m. *prosecutor*

accūso, 1, *accuse, prosecute*

ācer, ācris, ācre, adj. *active, drastic*

acerbē, adv. *cruelly, bitterly*

acervātim, adv. *in a mass, summarily*

actio, -ōnis, f. *hearing* (of a case)

acūtus, adj. *clever*

addo, 3, addidi, additum, *add*

addūco (dūco), *bring in*

adeo (eo), *approach, visit*

adeo, adv. *so, so greatly;* **adeo potius,** *nay rather*

adesset from **adsum,** *am present*

adhibeo, 2, *call in*

adhūc, adv. *so far, still*

aditus, -ūs, m. *approach, opportunity, attack*

adiungo, 3, adiunxi, adiunctum, *add, connect*

adiūtor, -ōris, m. *helper*

adiuvo, 1, -iūvi, -iūtum, *help*

administer, -tri, m. *agent*

admiror, 1, dep. *am surprised at*

admitto (mitto), *let in, commit*

admoveo, 2, admōvi, admōtum, *bring near, apply*

adorno, 1, *prepare, decorate*

adulescens, -entis, c. *young person*

adulescentia, -ae, f. *inexperience*

adulterīnus, adj. *forged*

aduncus, adj. *curved, hooked*

advoco, 1, *summon*

advolo, 1, *swoop down, attack*
aedes, -is, f. *temple*, plur. *house*
aedilitas, -ātis, f. *aedileship*
aegrōto, 1, *am ill*
aequābilis, adj. *consistent*
aequitas, -ātis, f. *justice, impartiality*
aequus, adj. *fair, just*
aerumnōsus, adj. *wretched, distressful*
aetas, -ātis, f. *age, time of life*
affero (fero), *convey, bring forward*
afficio (facio), *affect, reward, punish*
affinis, -is, c. *relation by marriage*
affligo, 3, afflixi, afflictum, *strike, harm*
affluo, 3, affluxi, affluxum, *overflow, reek with*
age, interj. *come now!*
ager, agri, m. *field, farm, territory*
aggredior, 3, aggressus, dep. *attack*
agito, 1, *consider, discuss*
ago, 3, ēgi, actum, *arrange, set about, plead a case*
aio, ais, ait, defect. verb, *I say*
Albiānus, adj. *belonging to Albius*
Alētrinās, -ātis, c. *of Aletrium*
aliquamdiū, adv. *for any length of time*
aliquando, adv. *at last*
aliquantum, -i, n. *a considerable amount*
aliquis, pron. *some one, some*
aliquot, indecl. adj. *several*
alius, pron. *another*, pl. *others*
alligātus, adj. *implicated, attached*

alloquor, 3, allocūtus, dep. *speak to*
altē, adv. *deeply, far*
alter, pron. *the one or the other*
amans, -antis, c. *lover*, or as adj. *loving*
amārus, adj. *bitter*
ambitio, -ōnis, f. *bribery, ambition*
āmens, -entis, adj. *mad*
āmentia, -ae, f. *folly, madness*
amīcitia, -ae, f. *friendship*
amīcus, adj. *friendly*; subst. *a friend*
amita, -ae, f. *aunt* (paternal)
āmitto, 3 (mitto), *lose*
amor, -ōris, m. *love, desire*
amplius, adv. *more*
an, conj. *or*, interrogative
Ancōnitānus, adj. *from Ancona*
ango, 3, anxi, anctum, *throttle, torture, vex*
animadverto, 3, -verti, -versum, *notice*
animus, -i, m. *disposition, character, thoughts, feelings*
annus, -i, m. *year*
ante, adv. or prep. *before*
anteā, adv. *before, formerly*
antequam, conj. *before, until*
aperio, 4, aperui, apertum, *open, disclose*
apertus, adj. *open, plain*
appello, 1, *call, name, appeal to*
applico, 1, *devote*
appropinquo, 1, *come near*
apud, prep. *at, near, among, at the house of*
Aquinās, -ātis, c. *of Aquinum*
āra, -ae, f. *altar*

72

arbitror, 1, dep. *think, decide*
arcesso, 3, arcessīvi, arcessī-
tum, *summon, fetch*
arēnāria, -ae, f. *sand-pit*
argūmentor, 1, dep. *argue,
discuss*
argūmentum, -i, n. *evidence*
armārium, -i, n. *chest, cup-
board*
armātus, -i, m. *armed man*
armo, 1, *arm*
ars, artis, f. *art, skill*
artificium, -i, n. *profession,
skill, art*
aspectus, -ūs, m. *aspect, glance*
aspergo, 3, aspersi, aspersum,
sprinkle
aspernor, 1, dep. *treat with
contempt, reject*
aspicio, 3, aspexi, aspectum,
look at
assentātio, -ōnis, f. *blandish-
ment, flattery*
assēvero, 1, *assert, proclaim*
assiduus, adj. *perpetual, un-
ending*
assimulātus, adj. *sham, pretended*
at, conj. *but, at any rate;* at
enim, *but some one may say*
atque, conj. *moreover, also,
straightway*
ātrōcitas, -ātis, f. *horribleness*
attamen, adv. *nevertheless*
attentē, adv. *attentively*
auctio, -ōnis, f. *sale*
auctor, -ōris, m. *backer, guardian*
auctōritas, -ātis, f. *authority,
influence*
audācia, -ae, f. *audacity, in-
solence*
audeo, 2, ausus, semi-dep. *dare*

audio, 4, *hear*
aufero, auferre, abstuli, ab-
lātum, *take away, recover*
augeo, 2, auxi, auctum, *increase, enlarge*
auris, -is, f. *ear*
aurum, -i, n. *gold*
auspex, auspicis, c. *soothsayer,
witness at a wedding*
autem, conj. *but, moreover,
well then, nay*
auxilium, -i, n. *aid*
āversor, 1, dep. *turn away*
(one's face)
avia, -ae, f. *grandmother*

bellum, -i, n. *war*
beneficium, -i, n. *kind action*
benevolus, adj. *well-disposed*
bestia, -ae, f. *wild beast*
bibo, 3, bibi, bibitum, *drink*
bis, adv. *twice*
blandē, adv. *winningly*
blanditia, -ae, f. *flattery, en-
ticement*
bona, n. pl. *property*
bonitas, -ātis, f. *good conduct*
bonus, adj. *good, honest*
brevis, adj. *short*
breviter, adv. *briefly*

C., abbrev. for Gāius
cado, 3, cecidi, cāsum, *fall*
caecus, adj. *blinded*
caedes, -is, f. *murder, slaughter*
calamitas, -ātis, f. *disaster,
harm*
callidē, adv. *cunningly*
candidātus, -i, m. *candidate*
capio, 3, capere, cēpi, captum,
take, charm, feel
caput, -itis, n. *head, life, civil
rights*

73

cārus, adj. *dear, beloved*
cāsus, -ūs, m. *chance, danger*
causa, -ae, f. *cause, case, reason, sake*
celebro, 1, *make famous, discuss*
censōrius, adj. *of the censor*
cerno, 3, crēvi, crētum, *perceive, see clearly*
certē, adv. *undoubtedly*
certus, adj. *certain, sure*
cēterī, -ōrum, adj. *the others*
circumforāneus, adj. *itinerant*
circumscriptio, -ōnis, f. *cheating, swindling*
circumseco, 1, -secui, -sectum, *cut out*
circumvenio (venio), *surround, condemn falsely*
cito, 1, *summon*
cīvis, -is, o. *citizen*
cīvitas, -ātis, f. *state, society*
clāmo, 1, *shout, complain*
clāmor, -ōris, m. *shout, cry*
clārus, adj. *clear, loud, famous*
clēmentia, -ae, f. *mercy*
Cluentiānus, adj. *of Cluentius*
coactor, -ōris, m. *money-collector*
coarguo, 3, *prove guilty, condemn*
coepī, coepisse, defective verb, *I begin*
cōgitātio, -ōnis, f. *reflection, meditation*
cōgito, 1, *think about, aspire to*
cognātio, -ōnis, f. *relationship, kin*
cognātus, -i, m. *relation*
cognōmen, -inis, n. *surname*
cognosco, 3, cognōvi, cognitum, *find out, know*

cōgo, 3, coēgi, coactum, *compel*
colliquefactus, adj. *completely dissolved*
collocātio, -ōnis, f. *giving in marriage*
collum, -i, n. *neck*
colōnus, -i, m. *farmer*
columna, -ae, f. *pillar*
combūro, 3, combussi, combustum, *burn up, cremate*
comedo, comesse, comēdi, comēsum or comestum, *eat*
comitātus, -ūs, m. *retinue, escort*
commemorātio, -ōnis, f. *record, remembrance*
committo (mitto), *entrust, act*
commodē, adv. *conveniently*
commodum, -i, n. *privilege, gift*
commoror, 1, dep. *linger*
commoveo, 2, -mōvi, -mōtum, *stir deeply, stir up against*
commūnico, 1, *confer with*
commūnis, adj. *common, mutual*
comparātio, -ōnis, f. *preparation*
compāreo, 2, *appear, come forward*
comparo, 1, *prepare*
comperio, 4, comperi, compertum, *ascertain*
comprehendo, 3, -prehendi, -prehensum, *ascertain, detect*
comprobo, 1, *approve, agree*
concordia, -ae, f. *agreement*
concupisco, 3, concupīvi, *desire greatly*
concursus, -ūs, m. *concourse*
condemno, 1, *condemn*

74

condio, 4, *pickle, season*
conditio, -ōnis, f. *condition, terms*
conditor, -ōris, m. *maker, author*
condo, 3, -didi, -ditum, *hide*
condōno, 1, *sacrifice to*
condūco (dūco), *collect, hire*
confero (fero), *collect, attach to;* sē contulit, *betook himself*
confestim, adv. *in haste*
conficio (facio), *complete*
confīdo, 3, confīsus, semi-dep. *trust*
confirmo, 1, *strengthen, encourage*
confiteor, 2, confessus, dep. *confess*
conflo, 1, *kindle, invent*
confugio (fugio), *take refuge, have recourse to*
confundo, 3, confūdi, confūsum, *mix*
congressio, -ōnis, f. *intercourse*
coniungo, 3, coniunxi, coniunctum, *combine* §1, *form* §13
cōnor, 1, dep. *attempt*
conquiro, 3, -quīsīvi, -quīsītum, *collect, procure*
conscelerātus, adj. *villainous, criminal*
conscisco, 3, conscīvi, conscītum, *decree;* mortem sibi, *commit suicide*
conscientia, -ae, f. *guilty share, guilty knowledge*
conscius, adj. *accessory, with the knowledge of*
conscrībo (scrībo), *write out, compose*
consenesco, 3, consenui, *become weak, pine away*

consequor, 3, consecūtus, dep. *stand to gain*
conservus, -i, m. *fellow-slave*
consilium, -i, n. *plan, wisdom, jury, court*
consisto, 3, constiti, *halt, remain*
consōbrīnus, -i, m. *cousin*
constans, -stantis, adj. *steady*
constantia, -ae, f. *consistency, firmness*
constat, impers. 1, *it is agreed*
constituo, 3, *decide, arrange, bring before the court*
consuesco, 3, consuēvi, consuētum, *am accustomed*
consuētūdo, -inis, f. *intimacy, habit*
consulto, 1, *consult, reflect*
consultō, adv. *purposely*
consurgo, 3, -surrexi, -surrectum, *rise together*
contāgio, -ōnis, f. *infection*
contāminātus, adj. *polluted, degenerate*
contendo, 3, contendi, contentum, *strive to obtain*
contineo, 2, -tinui, -tentum, *restrain; involve,* §24
continuō, adv. *straightway*
contio, -ōnis, f. *public meeting, mob oratory*
contrā, adv. *on the other hand,* prep. *against*
contraho, 3, -traxi, -tractum, *have dealings with;* with frontem, *to frown*
contrōversia, -ae, f. *dispute*
convalesco, 3, convalui, *get better, recover health*
conventus, -ūs, m. *assembly*
converto, 3, -verti, -versum, *change, turn*

75

convīcium, -i, n. *outcry, accusation*
convīva, -ae, c. *fellow, companion*
convīvium, -i, n. *feasting*
convoco, 1, *call together*
cōplōsē, adv. *fully*
cōram, adv. *face to face*
corpus, -oris, n. *body*
corrumpo, 3, corrūpi, corruptum, *corrupt, bribe*
crēdo, 3, crēdidi, crēditum, *believe*
crīmen, -inis, n. *accusation, crime, charge*
crūdēlis, adj. *brutal, cruel*
crūdēlitas, -ātis, f. *cruelty*
crūdēliter, adv. *cruelly*
crūdus, adj. *raw, suffering from indigestion*
crux, crūcis, f. *cross*
cubīle, -is, n. *bed, lair*
culpa, -ae, f. *blame, fault*
cum, conj. *when, since, although*
cum...tum, *not only...but also*
cumulus, -i, m. *heap, total*
cupiditas, -ātis, f. *desire, greed*
cupidus, adj. *desirous*
cupio, 3, cupere, cupīvi, cupītum, *desire, wish*
cūr, adv. *why*
cūro, 1, *take care of, look after, cause* (to be done)

damnātio, -ōnis, f. *condemnation*
damno, 1, *condemn*
dēbeo, 2, *owe, ought, am bound*
dēcēdo, 3, decessi, decessum, *withdraw, am subtracted from*
decem, indecl. adj. *ten*

dēclāro, 1, *make clear*
decurio, -ōnis, m. *councillor*
dēdecus, -oris, n. *disgrace, infamy*
dēdūco (dūco), *bring down*
dēfendo, 3, dēfendi, dēfensum, *defend*
dēfensio, -ōnis, f. *defence*
dēfero (fero), *bring down, report;* with nōmen, *inform against*
dēfessus, adj. *worn-out, weary*
dēficio (facio), *fail, am lacking*
dēgusto, 1, *taste*
deinde, conj. *afterwards, next*
dēlātio (nōminis), -ōnis, f. *accusation*
dēlēnio, 4, *captivate, soothe, persuade*
dēleo, 2, dēlēvi, dēlētum, *smudge, destroy*
dēligo, 3, dēlēgi, dēlectum, *choose*
dēmissus, adj. *downcast, despondent*
dēmonstro, 1, *show, prove*
dēnique, adv. *finally, in short*
dentātus, adj. *toothed*
dēnuntio, 1, *threaten*
dēnuo, adv. *afresh*
dēpello, 3, dēpuli, dēpulsum, *turn aside, thrust away*
dēplōro, 1, *lament*
dēprehendo, 3, dēprehendi, dēprehensum, *detect, find*
dēprōmo, 3, dēprompsi, dēpromptum, *produce*
dēsēro, 3, dēserui, dēsertum, *desert, abandon*
dēsīdero, 1, *require, am missing* (passive)
despondeo, 2, despondi, desponsum, *betroth*

76

destituo, 3, *abandon, leave in
the lurch*
destitūtio, -ōnis, f. *failure to
pay*
dēsum, dēesse, dēfui, *am
lacking*
dēterrimus, adj. *vile, degraded*
dētraho, 3, dētraxi, dētractum,
remove from, subtract
deus, -i, m. *god*
dēvincio, 4, dēvinxi, dēvin-
ctum, *oblige, enslave*
dico, 3, dixi, dictum, *say, tell*
dictito, 1, *assert repeatedly*
dies, -ēi, m. and f. *day, time*
difficilis, adj. *difficult*
diffido, 3, diffīsus, semi-dep.
have no faith in, despair of
digitus, -i, m. *finger*
dignitas, -ātis, f. *fitness, rank,
dignity*
dignus, adj. *worthy, deserving*
diligens, -entis, adj. *indus-
trious*
diligo, 3, dīlexi, dīlectum, *like,
love*
diluo, 3, *destroy*
dimitto (mitto), *send away,
postpone*
discēdo, 3, discessi, discessum,
leave, depart
disciplina, -ae, f. *training,
"school"*
discordia, -ae, f. *civil war,
quarrel*
discribo (scribo), *allot, divide*
dispertio, 4, *distribute*
disputo, 1, *discuss*
dissimilis, adj. *unlike*
dissolūtus, adj. *careless, dissolute*
diū, adv. *for a long time*
diūtius, adv. *any longer*

diūturnus, adj. *long-lasting*
divortium, -i, n. *divorce*
do, 1, dedi, datum, *give*
dolor, -ōris, m. *grief, pain,
resentment*
domesticus, adj. *belonging to
the house, inside*
domina, -ae, f. *mistress*
domus, -ūs, f. *house, home*
dōnum, -i, n. *gift*
dormio, 4, *sleep*
dubitātio, -ōnis, f. *doubt,
hesitation*
dubito, 1, *doubt*
dubius, adj. *doubtful, un-
certain*
dūco, 3, duxi, ductum, *lead,
marry, reckon*
dum, conj. *while, until, so
long as*
dūrus, adj. *hard, cruel*

ē, ex, prep. *from, out of, in
accordance with*
ecce, interj. *lo! behold!*
ecquid, int. pron. *won't you?*
ēdo, 3, ēdidi, ēditum, *give out,
publish*
ēduco, 1, *bring up* (a child)
efficio (facio), *carry out, execute*
effrēnātus, adj. *unbridled*
egens, egentis, adj. *needy*
egestas, -ātis, f. *want, destitution*
ēgregius, adj. *excellent, wonderful, best of*
ēicio, 3, eicere, ēiēci, ēiectum,
expel, banish
eiusmodi, *of that sort*
ēloquens, -entis, adj. *eloquent*
ēloquentia, -ae, f. *eloquence*
emo, 3, ēmi, emptum, *buy*
ēmorior (morior), *die* (at once)

77

ēn, interj. *behold!*
enim, conj. *for, indeed*
ēnumerātio, -ōnis, f. *detailed statement*
eo, īre, īvi, itum, *go*
eo, adv. *thither, to such a degree*
eōdem, eundem, see idem
ēpōtus, adj. *swallowed, drunk up*
equus, -i, m. *horse*
ergastulum, -i, n. *private prison, slave-house*
ērigo, 3, ērexi, ērectum, *rouse up, lift*
ēripio, 3, ēripere, ēripui, ēreptum, *snatch away, deprive*
Esquilīnus, one of the seven hills of Rome
etenim, conj. *for indeed*
etiam, conj. *also, even*
etsī, conj. *although*
exanimātus, adj. *half-dead, grief-stricken*
excito, 1, *excite, stir up*
exclūdo, 3, exclūsi, exclūsum, *shut out*
excōgito, 1, *devise, plan*
exemplum, -i, n. *example*
exerceo, 2, *practise*
exercitātus, adj. *experienced*
exhaurio, 4, exhausi, exhaustum, *drink up*
existimātio, -ōnis, f. *opinion, reputation*
existimo, 1, *think, estimate*
exitus, -ūs, m. *outcome, end*
exorior (orior), *spring up, show oneself*
exōro, 1, *persuade (by entreaty)*
experiens, -entis, adj. *enterprising*

expers, -ertis, adj. *without a share (in)*
expīlo, 1, *rob*
expio, 1, *purify*
expleo, 2, explēvi, explētum, *satisfy*
expōno (pōno), *set forth, explain*
expugno, 1, *take by siege, seize*
exseco, 1, exsecui, exsectum, *cut out*
exsectio, -ōnis, f. *cutting out*
exsequiae, -ārum, f. *funeral rites*
exsilium, -i, n. *banishment*
exspectātio, -ōnis, f. *waiting to see, speculation*
exspecto, 1, *wait for*
exsul, exsulis, c. *an exile*
exsulto, 1, *leap, exult, boast, rejoice*
exsurgo, 3, exsurrexi, exsurrectum, *stand up*
extorqueo, 2, extorsi, extortum, *wrench away, extort*
extrā, prep. *outside*
extraho, 3, extraxi, extractum, *drag out*
extrēmus, adj. *furthest, the end of*

Fābrāternus, adj. *belonging to Fabrateria*
Fābriciānus, adj. *belonging to Fabricius*
fābula, -ae, f. *tale, fable*
facies, -ēi, f. *face, appearance*
facile, adv. *easily, quite*
facilis, adj. *easy*
facinus, -oris, n. *deed, crime*
facio, 3, facere, fēci, factum, *do, make, appoint, cause*

fallo, 3, fefelli, falsum, *deceive,*
escape notice
falsus, adj. *false, trumped up*
fāma, -ae, f. *report, public*
opinion, fame
familia, -ae, f. *household,*
family
famllīāris, -is, m. *servant,*
friend
famllīārītas, -ātis, f. *friendship*
famllīārīter, adv. *intimately*
fās, indecl. n. *divine law, what*
is right
fateor, 2, fassus, dep. *confess*
fautor, -ōris, m. *supporter*
febris, -is, f. *fever*
fēmina, -ae, f. *woman*
ferē, adv. *almost, generally*
fero, ferre, tuli, lātum, *bring,*
bear, relate; sententiam
ferre, *to vote*
festus, adj. *festal;* dies festi,
holidays
fidēlis, adj. *faithful*
fides, -ēi, f. *faith, honour,*
loyalty
fīlia, -ae, f. *daughter*
fīlius, -i, m. *son*
fingo, 3, finxi, fictum, *feign,*
invent
finis, -is, m. *end*
firmo, 1, *strengthen, fix*
firmus, adj. *strong*
flāgitium, -i, n. *crime, pro-*
fligacy
flāgito, 1, *insist on, demand*
flagro, 1, *am inflamed with,*
burn
flamma, -ae, f. *flame, scorching*
fleo, 2, flēvi, flētum, *weep*
flētus, -ūs, m. *weeping, tears*
fore, *future infinitive of* sum
forma, -ae, f. *appearance, looks*

fortasse, adv. *perhaps*
forte, adv. *by chance*
fortis, adj. *strong, vigorous,*
brave
forum, -i, n. *market place,*
forum
frāter, frātris, m. *brother*
frāternus, adj. *of a brother*
fraus, fraudis, f. *deceit, trea-*
chery
frequentia, -ae, f. *crowd*
frons, frontis, f. *forehead*
fructus, -ūs, m. *fruit, reward*
frūgī, indecl. adj. *honest*
fruor, 3, fructus *or* fruitus,
dep. *enjoy*
fuga, -ae, f. *flight*
fugio, 3, fūgi, fugitum, *flee,*
avoid
fundāmentum, -i, n. *founda-*
tion
fundus, -i, m. *bottom*
fūnestus, adj. *fatal, sinister*
fūnus, -eris, n. *funeral rites,*
burial
furiōsus, adj. *frenzied*
furo, 3, *am mad*
furor, -ōris, m. *madness, mad*
folly
furtum, -i, n. *theft*

gaudeo, 2, gāvisus, semi-dep.
rejoice
gaudium, -i, n. *joy*
geminus, -i, m. *twin*
gemitus, -ūs, m. *groan*
gener, -i, m. *son-in-law*
genus, -eris, n. *kind, race, birth*
gero, 3, gessi, gestum, *do,*
carry out
grandis, adj. *tall, large, full-*
grown
grātia, -ae, f. *favour, influence*

79

grātīs, adv. *for nothing, with-out pay*
gravidus, adj. *laden, with child, pregnant*
gravis, adj. *important, severe*
graviter, adv. *heavily;* g. ferre, *to resent*
gravor, 1, dep. *am annoyed, troubled*
gremium, -i, n. *lap, bosom;* manibus et gremio, *embrace*

habeo, 2, *have, hold, reckon, make a speech*
hērēditas, -ātis, f. *inheritance*
hērēs, -ēdis, c. *heir*
hīc, adv. *here, hereupon*
hīc, haec, hōc, pron. *this*
hicce, emphatic form of hīc, pron.
hilarus, adj. *cheerful*
homo, -inis, c. *man, human being*
honestus, adj. *honourable, virtuous*
honor, -ōris, m. *position of honour, an honour*
hōra, -ae, f. *hour, time, season*
hortulus, -i, m. *garden*
hospes, -itis, c. *guest, friend*
hostia, -ae, f. *victim, sacrifice*
hostīlīs, adj. *hostile, cruel*
hostis, -is, c. *enemy*
hūc, adv. *hither*
hūmānitas, -ātis, f. *kindness, decent feelings*

iactūra, -ae, f. *loss, cost*
iam, adv. *now, already, soon*
iamdiū, adv. *for some time*
ibi, adv. *there*
idcirco, adv. *for that reason*

idem, eadem, idem, pron. *same*
igitur, conj. *therefore, so then*
ignārus, adj. *ignorant, not informed of*
ignōbilis, adj. *obscure*
ignōro, 1, *am ignorant*
ille, pron. *that, that man*
illico, adv. *immediately*
imāgo, -inis, f. *portrait, bust*
immānis, adj. *monstrous, in-human*
immergo, 3, immersī, immersum, *plunge in., creep into*
immortālis, adj. *immortal*
impello, 3, impuli, impulsum, *push over, nudge*
impendeo, 2, *overhang, threaten*
impero, 1, *command*
impius, adj. *wicked*
importūnitas, -ātis, f. *wickedness*
importūnus, adj. *shameless*
improbitas, -ātis, f. *dishonesty, vile conduct*
improbus, adj. *incorrigible, bold, wicked*
imprūdentia, -ae, f. *ignorance*
impudens, -entis, adj. *shameless*
impudenter, adv. *shamelessly*
impudentia, -ae, f. *impudence*
impūrus, adj. *infamous*
in, prep. *in, on, into, against*
inānis, adj. *poverty-stricken, empty*
inaudītus, adj. *unheard of, unheard*
incallidus, adj. *stupid*
incendo, 3, incendi, incensum, *set on fire, excite*

incertus, adj. *doubtful, hesitating*
incido, 3, incidi, *fall into, fall in with*
incipio (capio), *begin*
incognitus, adj. *unknown*
incolumis, adj. *safe, unpunished, unimpaired*
inconstantia, -ae, f. *inconsistency*
incrēdibilis, adj. *unbelievable*
incubo, 1, incubui, incubitum, *watch over, brood upon*
index, -icis, m. *informer, guide*
indicium, -i, n. *sign, evidence*
indico, 1, *point out, discover*
indignē, adv. *undeservedly*
indomitus, adj. *untamed, ungovernable*
indūco (dūco), with animum, *bring one's self to*
industrius, adj. *diligent, busy*
ineo (eo), *go in, make a plan*
ineptiae, -ārum, f. *absurdities*
inermis, adj. *unarmed*
infāmia, -ae, f. *infamy, disgrace*
infans, -antis, c. *baby, young child*
inferus, adj. *below*; apud inferos, *in the world below*
infestus, adj. *hostile*
infinitus, adj. *endless*
infirmus, adj. *weak*
inicio, 3, inicere, iniēci, iniectum, *throw in*; passive, *occur to*
inimicitia, -ae, f. *enmity*
inimicus, -i, m. (private) *enemy*
iniquus, adj. *hostile*
initium, -i, n. *beginning*

iniūria, -ae, f. *wrong, injury, affront*
innocens, -entis, adj. *innocent*
inopia, -ae, f. *want, destitution*
inquam, inquit, *I say, says he*
inquiro, 3, -quisivi, -quisitum, *search into, scrutinize*
insequor, 3, insecūtus, dep. *pursue, reproach*
insidiae, -ārum, f. *plot, trickery*
insimulo, 1, *charge, accuse*
instituo, 3, *begin, appoint*
instruo, 3, -struxi, -structum, *furnish, instruct*
integer, integra, integrum, adj. *whole, sound*; dē integro, *anew, all over again*
intellego, 3, -lexi, -lectum, *understand*
inter, prep. *between, among during*
intercēdo, 3, -cessi, -cessum, *come between, pass*
interceptio, -ōnis, f. *interception*
intercipio (capio), *intercept*
interdum, adv. *at times*
interficio (facio), *put to death*
interim, adv. *meanwhile*
interitus, -ūs, m. *death, destruction*
intervallum, -i, n. *interval*
intervenio (venio), *am present*
intimus, adj. *inmost*
intrā, prep. and adv. *within*
intrōdūco (dūco), *bring in*
intueor, 2, intuitus, dep. *gaze upon*
inultus, adj. *unavenged, unpunished*
inūsitātus, adj. *uncommon*
invādo, 3, -vāsi, -vāsum, *rush upon, lay hold of*

invenio (venio), *find*
investīgo, 1, *look for, find*
invideo (video), *envy, grudge*
invidia, -ae, f. *unpopularity,
     prejudice*
invītus, adj. *unwilling*
ipse, pron. *self*
īrātus, adj. *enraged*
iste, pron. *that of yours*
istinc, adv. *on that side, thence*
ita, adv. *so, thus, on this con-
     dition*
itaque, conj. *therefore*
item, adv. *likewise, also*
iterum, adv. *again, for the
     second time*
iubeo, 2, iussi, iussum, *order,
     bid*
iūcundus, adj. *pleasing*
iūdex, -icis, c. *judge, juryman*
iūdiciārius, adj. *obtained from
     the law courts*
iūdicium, -i, n. *trial, judgment*
iūdico, 1, *declare, consider*
iūro, 1, *am bound by an oath*
iūs, iūris, n. *right, law, insti-
     tution*
iustē, adv. *justly*
iustus, adj. *just, proper*

L., abbrev. for Lūcius
labefacto, 1, *weaken, under-
     mine*
labor, -ōris, m. *trouble*
labōro, 1, *suffer*
lacrima, -ae, f. *tear*
laedo, 3, laesi, laesum, *hurt,
     damage*
laetor, 1, dep. *rejoice*
Lārīnas, -ātis, c. *of Larinum*
lātē, adv. *widely*
lateo, 2, *lie hid*
latito, 1, *lurk*

lātus, partic. of fero
latus, -eris, n. *side, ribs*
lēgātum, -i, n. *legacy*
lēgo, 1, *leave by will*
lēniter, adv. *gently*
levis, adj. *light, fickle, in-
     significant*
leviter, adv. *lightly, gently*
levo, 1, *raise, save*
lex, lēgis, f. *law*
libenter, adv. *gladly, cheerfully*
liberi, -ōrum, and liberum,
     m. *children, freeborn sons*
libero, 1, *set free*
libertus, -i, m. *a slave who has
     been set free, a freedman*
libīdo, -inis, f. *passion, lust,
     caprice*
Ligur, -uris, c. *a Ligurian*
lingua, -ae, f. *tongue*
liqueo, 2, *am clear*; impersonal
     use, non liquet, *it is not
     proved*
littera, -ae, f. *letter of the
     alphabet*
litterae, -ārum, f. *letter, epistle*
litūra, -ae, f. *smudge, oblitera-
     tion*
locus, -i, m. *place*
longus, adj. *long, tedious*
loquax, -ācis, adj. *talkative*
loquor, 3, locūtus, dep. *speak*
lūceo, 2, *shine*; impersonal
     use, lucet, *it dawns*
luctus, -ūs, m. *sorrow, cause of
     grief*
lūdus, -i, m. *game, school*;
     plur. *public games*
lūgeo, 2, luxi, *mourn*

M., abbrev. for Marcus
māchina, -ae, f. *engine-of-
     war*

82

macula, -ae, f. *blot, stain, disgrace*
maereo, 2, *grieve*
maeror, -ōris, m. *grief, mourning*
magis, adv. *more, rather*
magnus, adj. *great*
mālor, adj. *greater, elder*
maleficium, -i, n. *ill-doing*
malitia, -ae, f. *iniquity*
mālo, mālle, mālui, *prefer*
malum, -i, n. *evil, misfortune*
malus, adj. *bad, evil*
maneo, 2, mansi, mansum, *remain*
manifesto, adv. *plainly, without doubt*
manifestus, adj. *clear, plain*
māno, 1, *leak out*
manus, -ūs, f. *hand, arm, power*
mare, -is, n. *sea*
māter, matris, f. *mother*
mātrimōnium, -i, n. *marriage*
mātūro, 1, *hasten, accelerate*
medicāmentum, -i, n. *cure*
medicīna, -ae, f. *medicine, drug*
medicus, -i, m. *physician*
mediocris, adj. *moderate*
meditātio, -ōnis, f. *meditation*
medius, adj. *middle*
melius, adv. *better*
memini, meminisse, *remember*
memoria, -ae, f. *memory*
mendācium, -i, n. *falsehood*
mendax, mendācis, adj. *deceitful*
mens, mentis, f. *mind, thoughts*
mentio, -ōnis, f. *mention*
mentior, 4, dep. *tell lies*
metuo, 3, *fear*
metus, -ūs, m. *fear, apprehension*

mille, indecl. adj. *a thousand;* pl. mīlia
minae, -ārum, f. *threats*
minimē, adv. *far from, by no means*
minister, -tri, m. *agent*
minor, adj. *less, younger*
minor, 1, dep. *threaten*
minūtus, adj. *small, unimportant*
miror, 1, dep. *wonder, be surprised*
mirus, adj. *wonderful;* nec mirum, *and no wonder*
miser, adj. *wretched, poor*
miseria, -ae, f. *misery, misfortune*
misericordia, -ae, f. *pity*
mitto, 3, misi, missum, *send*
moderātus, adj. *orderly*
modo, adv. *only*
modus, -i, m. *manner, limit, restraint*
molestia, -ae, f. *trouble, worry*
molestus, adj. *painful*
mōlior, 4, dep. *build up, plan*
monstrum, -i, n. *monster, horror*
mora, -ae, f. *delay, hindrance*
morbus, -i, m. *illness, disease*
mōres, -um, m. *character*
morior, mori, mortuus, dep. *die*
moror, 1, dep. *dwell, delay*
mors, mortis, f. *death*
mortālis, -is, m. *man, person*
mōs, mōris, m. *custom*
muliebris, adj. *feminine, womanly*
mulier, -eris, f. *woman, wife*
mulsum, -i, n. [vinum understood], *wine and honey*
multitūdo, -inis, f. *crowd, quantity*

83

multo, 1, *fine, punish*
multo, adv. *much*
multum, adv. *much*
multus, adj. *much, many*
mūniceps, -cipis, c. *townsman*
mūnicipium, -i, n. *country town*
mūnio, 4, *build up, prepare the way*
mūnus, -eris, n. *duty, gift*
mūto, 1, *alter*

nam, conj. *for*
nascor, 3, nātus, dep. *am born, spring from*
nātio, -ōnis, f. *nation, tribe*
nātūra, -ae, f. *nature*
nātus, with annos, *old*; with abl. *son of*
nē (nae), *verily*
nē, conj. *lest, that . . . not*
nē . . . quidem, *not even*
necessārius, adj. *necessary*; subst. *friend, relation*
necesse, indecl. adj. *inevitable*
necessitas, -ātis, f. *privation, poverty*
necessitūdo, -inis, f. *relationship*
neco, 1, *kill*
nefārius, adj. *wicked, abominable*
neglegenter, adv. *slackly*
nego, 1, *deny*
negōtium, -i, n. *task, business*
nēmo, c. *nobody, not one*
nempe, conj. *namely, to wit*
nepōs, -ōtis, m. *grandson*
nēquāquam, adv. *by no means*
nēquitia, -ae, f. *vileness, villainy*
nescioquis, pron. *some one or other*

nihil, indecl. n. *nothing*; nihil mali, *no harm*; adv. *in no respect*
nihilōminus, adv. *none the less*
nimium, adv. *too, too much*
nisi, conj. *unless, except, if . . . not*
nōbilis, adj. *well-born, renowned*
nōbilitas, -ātis, f. *renown, birth*
nocens, -entis, adj. *guilty*
noctū, adv. *by night*
nocturnus, adj. *done by night*
nōlo, nolle, nōlui, *refuse*
nōmen, -inis, n. *name, clan, fame*
nōmino, 1, *name*
nondum, adv. *not yet*
nonne, interrogative particle
nonnulli, pl. adj. *some*
nosco, 3, nōvi, nōtum, *know (a person)*
nostrum, genit. pl. of ego
nōtus, adj. *well-known*
noverca, -ae, f. *stepmother*
novus, adj. *new, fresh, strange*
nox, noctis, f. *night*
nūbilis, adj. *marriageable*
nūbo, 3, nupsi, nuptum, *marry* (female subject only)
nullus, adj. *no, none*
num, interrogative particle
Num., abbrev. for Numerius
numerus, -i, m. *number*
nummārius, adj. *bribed, venal*
nummus, -i, m. *coin*; genit. pl. nummum or nummōrum
numquam, adv. *never*
numquis, pron. *[does] anyone?*
nuntio, 1, *announce*
nūper, adv. *recently*
nuptiae, -ārum, f. *wedding, marriage feast*

84

nuptiālis, adj. *connected with a wedding*

ob, prep. *on account of*
obeo (eo), *meet*
obicio, 3, obicere, obiēci, obiectum, *cast up*
obscūrítas, -ātis, f. *obscurity*
obscūrus, adj. *hidden, dark, low*
obsecro, 1, *entreat*
obses, obsidis, c. *hostage, pledge*
obsignātor, -ōris, m. *witness to a will*
obsigno, 1, *seal, sign*
obstringo, 3, obstrinxi, obstrictum, *bind*
obtortus, adj. *twisted*; collo obtorto, *by the scruff of the neck*
occido, 3, occīdi, occīsum, *kill, murder*
occulto, 1, *conceal*
occultus, adj. *hidden, secret*
oculus, -i, m. *eye*
ōdi, ōdisse, defect. verb, *hate*
odium, -i, n. *hatred, disgust*
odor, -ōris, m. *smell, taint*
odōror, 1, dep. *smell out, track down*
offendo, 3, offendi, offensum, *meet with, find, bruise*
offensio, -ōnis, f. *failure, dislike*
offensus, adj. *odious*
offero (fero), *bestow, inflict*
ōmen, -inis, n. *omen, sign, prediction*
omitto (mitto), *leave out*
omnino, adv. *altogether*
omnis, adj. *all, every, the whole*
opinio, -ōnis, f. *judgment*

opprimo (premo), *crush, overcome, surprise*
oppugnātio, -ōnis, f. *attack*
oppugno, 1, *attack, assail*
optātus, adj. *longed for*
optimus, adj. *best, chief*
opto, 1, *wish, choose*
opus, -eris, n. *work, trouble*
opus est, with abl. *there is need*
ōrātio, -ōnis, f. *speech*
orbātus, adj. *deprived, bereaved*
orior, 4, ortus, dep. *arise, spring up*
ornātus, adj. *distinguished*
orno, 1, *furnish, adorn*
ōro, 1, *beg*
ōs, ōris, n. *mouth, words*
oscito, 1, *yawn*
ostendo, 3, ostendi, ostentum and ostensum, *show*
ostento, 1, *offer, hold out, threaten*

P., abbrev. for Publius
paene, adv. *almost*
palam, adv. *openly*
pānis, -is, m. *bread*
parco, 3, peperci, parsum or parcitum, *spare*
parens, -entis, c. *parent*
pariēs, -etis, m. *wall* (between rooms)
parricīdium, -i, n. *murder of a near relation*
pars, partis, f. *side, part*
partior, 4, dep. *share, divide*
partus, -ūs, m. *birth, delivery*
parum, adv. *too little, far from*
parvus, adj. *small*
pasco, 3, pāvi, pastum, *feed, nourish*
passus, -ūs, m. *step*; mille passūs, *a mile*

85

patefacio (facio), *lay open,
disclose*
pater, patris, m. *father*
patrius, adj. *of a father, inherited*
patrōnus, -i, m. *defender,
advocate*
pauci, pl. adj. *few*
paullisper, adv. *for a short time*
paullo, adv. *a little*
paullum, adv. *for a time*
pecūnia, -ae, f. *money*
pecūniōsus, adj. *rich*
pēlex, -icis, c. *rival*
pēlicātus, -ūs, m. *rivalry,
immorality*
pellicio, 3, -lexi, -lectum,
entice, win over
penitus, adv. *deeply*
per, prep. *through, by means of*
percontātio, -ōnis, f. *inquiry,
questioning*
percūriōsus, adj. *very in-
quisitive*
percurro, 3, -cucurri, -cursum,
run through, touch lightly on
perditus, adj. *abandoned, de-
sperate*
perdo, 3, -didi, -ditum, *lose,
destroy*
perdūco (dūco), *bring along*
pereo (eo), *perish, die*
perfero (fero), *endure*
perficio (facio), *carry out, bring
to pass*
perfidiōsus, adj. *treacherous*
perfringo, 3, -frēgi, -fractum,
break through, shatter, violate
perfugium, -i, n. *escape*
periculum, -i, n. *danger, action-
at-law*
perinde ut, conj. *just as*
perītus, adj. *experienced*
permagnus, adj. *enormous*

permāno, 1, *spread through,
penetrate*
pernicies, -ēi, f. *destruction,
death*
perniciōsus, adj. *deadly, baleful*
pernocto, 1, *stay the night*
perōro, 1, *finish a speech*
perpetuus, adj. *long-lasting;*
in perpetuum, *for ever*
perquīro, 3, -quīsīvi, -quīsī-
tum, *make inquiries*
persequor, 3, -secūtus, dep.
pursue
perspicio, 3, -spexi, -spectum,
see clearly, scrutinize
persuādeo, 2, -suāsi, -suāsum,
persuade
pertenuis, adj. *very thin, very
slight*
perterritus, adj. *terrified*
pertimesco, 3, -timui, *become
alarmed*
pertineo, 2, -tinui, -tentum,
belong to, am concerned with
pervenio (venio), *arrive, reach*
perversus, adj. *crooked, evil*
pēs, pedis, m. *foot*
pestis, -is, f. *pestilence, curse*
peto, 3, petīvi, petītum, *seek,
beg of, make for*
petulans, -antis, adj. *impudent*
pharmacopōla, -ae, m. *drug-
seller*
piē, adv. see pietas
pietas, -ātis, f. *dutifulness towards gods, country, or
family; piety, patriotism,
affection*
piscīna, -ae, f. *pond*
pius, adj. see pietas
placeo, 2, *please;* impersonal,
placet, *it is decided*

86

plăco, 1, *appease, reconcile*
plănē, adv. *easily, without in-*
quiry
planus, -i, m. *vagabond, jug-*
gler
plebs, plēbis, f. *the people*
plēnus, adj. *full, mature*
plērīque, pl. adj. *most*
plūrimus, adj. *very much, most*
plūs, plūris, n. *more*
pōculum, -i, n. *cup, drink,*
poison
Poena, -ae, f. *avenging deity*
poena, -ae, f. *penalty*
polliceor, 2, dep. *promise*
pondo, indecl. n. *weight, pound*
pōno, 3, posui, positum, *put,*
consider, rest upon
populus, -i, m. *the people*
porro, adv. *moreover, again*
porta, -ae, f. *gate, door*
portentum, -i, n. *monster,*
fiend
posco, 3, poposci, *demand*
possum, posse, potui, *am able,*
am powerful, can
post, adv. and prep. *after*
posteā, adv. *afterwards*
posteāquam, conj. *after*
posterus, adj. *following*
postrēmo, adv. *lastly, finally*
postrēmum, adv. *for the last*
time
postrīdiē, adv. *on the next day*
postulo, 1, *ask, demand*
potestas, -ātis, f. *power, skill,*
authority, right
potissimum, adv. *especially*
potius, adv. *rather*
praeceps, praecipitis, adj.
headlong
praecipito, 1, *fall, totter on the*
brink

praeclārus, adj. *splendid*
praeditus, adj. *endowed with,*
possessing
praeiūdicium, -i, n. *former*
conviction
praeiūdico, 1, *judge before*
praemium, -i, n. *profit*
praeposterus, adj. *topsy-turvy,*
perverse
praesens, -entis, adj. *face to*
face, present
praesertim, adv. *especially*
praeter, prep. *except, beside*
praftereā, adv. *moreover, be-*
sides
praetereo (eo), *omit, pass by*
praevāricor, 1, dep. *help the*
enemy, act in collusion
prandeo, 2, prandi, pransum,
dine
prandium, -i, n. *dinner*
prehendo, 3, prehendi, pre-
hensum, *seize*
premo, 3, pressi, pressum, *rest*
upon, pursue, hide
pretium, -i, n. *bribe, price*
[prex], f. pl. preces, *prayers,*
curses
prīmō, adv. *first, at first*
prīmum, adv. *in the first place*
princeps, principis, c. *first,*
chief, leader
principium, -i, n. *outset, begin-*
ning
pristinus, adj. *former, old-*
fashioned
prius, adv. *before*
priusquam, conj. *before, until*
prīvātus, adj. *private*
prīvo, 1, *deprive*
prō!, exclamation, o, *forbid!*
prō, prep. *before, in proportion*
to, for, because of

probābilis, adj. *credible*
probo, 1, *prove, approve*
prōcēdo, 3, -cessi, -cessum, *go forward, succeed*
profectio, -ōnis, f. *origin*
profecto, adv. *assuredly*
prōfero (fero), *bring forth*
prōficio (facio), *gain*
profugio (fugio), *flee away*
profūsus, adj. *lavish*
prohibeo, 2, *prevent*
prōmissum, -i, n. *promise*
prōnuntiātio, -ōnis, f. *verdict*
prooemium, -i, n. *introduction, preface*
prope, adv. and prep. *near, nearly*
propero, 1, *hurry*
propinquus, adj. *near;* as subst. *kinsman*
propior, adj. *nearer, closer*
prōpōno (pōno), *set before, give a task to*
propter, prep. *on account of, for;* adv. *near, at hand*
prōscrībo (scrībo), *outlaw*
prōscriptio, -ōnis, f. *outlawry*
prōsequor, 3, -secūtus, dep. *attend*
prosterno, 3, -strāvi, -strātum, *lay low, overthrow*
prūdentia, -ae, f. *wisdom, sagacity*
publicus, adj. *public, common*
pudīcitia, -ae, f. *modesty, purity, chastity*
pudor, -ōris, m. *shame, sense of shame, disgrace*
puer, pueri, m. *boy*
pueritia, -ae, f. *boyhood*
pulchrē, adv. *finely, splendidly* (often ironical)
punctum, -i, n. *dot, moment*

puto, 1, *think, suppose*

Q., abbrev. for Quintus
quadrāgēni, pl. adj. *forty each*
quaero, 3, quaesīvi, quaesītum, *seek, ask, gain*
quaeso, *I beg*
quaestio, -ōnis, f. *inquiry, court*
quaestus, -ūs, m. *gain, profit*
quam, adv. *how*
quam, conj. *than*
quamobrem, adv. *wherefore, why*
quamquam, conj. *although*
quantus, adj. *how great, what*
quārē, adv. *wherefore*
quasi, conj. *as though, as if*
quattuorviri, -ōrum, m. *council of four*
quemadmodum, adv. *just as, how*
querimōnia, -ae, f. *complaint, grievance*
queror, 3, questus, dep. *complain*
quia, conj. *because*
quicunque, pron. *whoever, whatever*
quid?, adv. *again, why?*
quidam, pron. *a certain, someone*
quidem, adv. *even, indeed*
quiesco, 3, quiēvi, quiētum, *rest, keep quiet*
quin, conj. with subj. *that;* with indic. *moreover*
quisnam, pron. *who, pray?*
quisquam, pron. *anyone*
quisque, pron. *each*
quisquis, pron. *whoever, whatever*
quod, conj. *because*

88

quodsī, conj. *now if, for if*
quondam, adv. *formerly*
quoniam, conj. *since, because*
quotīdiānus, adj. *daily*
quotīdiē, adv. *every day*

ratio, -ōnis, f. *understanding, reason, business, plot, way*
recens, recentis, adj. *recent*
recipio (capio,) *receive, take back*
recito, 1, *read aloud*
recordor, 1, dep. *recollect*
recupero, 1, *recover, get back*
recūso, 1, *refuse, shrink from*
reddo, 3, reddidi, redditum, *restore, render*
redūco (dūco), *lead back*
redundo, 1, *am soaked with*
reformīdo, 1, *shrink from*
regio, -ōnis, f. *district, neighbourhood*
rēligio, -ōnis, f. *worship, rites*
relinquo, 3, relīqui, relictum, *leave behind, abandon*
reliquus, adj. *remaining, the rest*
remaneo, 2, remansi, *remain*
remedium, -i, n. *remedy*
remōtus, adj. *far from, unlike*
renuntio, 1, *report*
repente, adv. *suddenly*
repentīnus, adj. *sudden*
reperio, 4, repperi, repertum, *find, discover*
repeto, 3, repetīvi, repetītum, *claim, ask to be given back*
repudio, 1, *scorn, reject*
reservo, 1, *retain, preserve*
respicio, respicere, respexi, respectum, *look at, look favourably on*
respiro, 1, *breathe freely, recover from*

respondeo, 2, respondi, responsum, *reply*
restituo, 3, *restore*
resto, 1, restiti, *remain*
retardo, 1, *impede, check*
reticeo, 2, *keep silence, conceal*
reus, -i, m. *accused person, defendant*
revertor, 3, dep. *come back*
revoco, 1, *recall, deter*
rīdeo, 2, rīsi, rīsum, *laugh*
rūmor, -ōris, m. *rumour, report*

sacrifīcium, -i, n. *sacrifice*
saepe, adv. *often*
salūs, -ūtis, f. *safety*
salvus, adj. *safe*
sanguis, -inis, m. *blood*
sapiens, -entis, adj. *wise*
satis, indecl. n. *enough;* adv. *very, quite*
satisfacio (facio), *satisfy, pay the debt to*
Scamander, -dri, m. *Scamander*
scelerātus, adj. *criminal*
scelus, -eris, n. *crime*
scio, 4, *know* (a fact)
scrībo, 3, scripsi, scriptum, *write, appoint*
scrūpulus, -i, m. *twenty-fourth part of an ounce, scruple, doubt*
scurra, -ae, m. *parasite, dinerout*
sēcerno, 3, sēcrēvi, sēcrētum, *separate*
sēdes, -is, f. *abode*
sēdulo, adv. *with the best intentions*
semel, adv. *once*
senātor, -ōris, m. *senator*
senectūs, -ūtis, f. *old age*

89

sensus, -ūs, m. *feeling, per-*
ception
sententia, -ae, f. *verdict, vote,*
opinion
sentio, 4, sensi, sensum, *feel,*
perceive
sepello, 4, sepelīvi, sepultum,
bury
sepulchrum, -i, n. *tomb, burial*
sequester, -tris, m. *depositary,*
trustee, agent
sermo, -ōnis, m. *speech, con-*
versation, gossip
sēro, adv. *too late*
serrula, -ae, f. *small saw*
servio, 4, *serve*
servitūs, -ūtis, f. *slavery*
servo, 1, *preserve, save*
servulus, -i, m. *serving-lad*
servus, -i, m. *slave*
sevērē, adv. *sternly*
sevērus, adj. *stern*
Sex., abbrev. for **Sextus**
sīc, adv. *thus*
sīcārius, -i, m. *assassin*
sīcut or sīcutī, conj. *as, just as*
significātio, -ōnis, f. *expression,*
uttering
signum, -i, n. *seal, signature*
silentium, -i, n. *silence*
sī minus, conj. *if not, not to*
mention
similis, adj. *like*
similitūdo, -inis, f. *likeness,*
similarity
simplex, simplicis, adj. *simple,*
clear
simul, adv. *together, at the*
same time
simul atque, conj. *as soon as*
simulo, 1, *pretend*
simultas, -ātis, f. *animosity,*
quarrel

sīn, conj. *but if*
sine, prep. *without*
singulāris, adj. *unique, un-*
paralleled
singulī, adj., plur. *only, one*
by one
sino, 3, sīvi, situm, *allow*
sinus, -ūs, m. *bosom*
sīve...sīve, conj. *whether...*
or
socrus, -ūs, f. *mother-in-law*
sodālis, -is, c. *companion*
sōlātium, -i, n. *relief, con-*
solation
soleo, 2, solitus, dep. *am wont,*
do usually
sollicitātio, -ōnis, f. *instigation*
sollicito, 1, *tempt*
sollicitūdo, -inis, f. *anxiety,*
trouble
sōlum, adv. *only*
sōlus, adj. *alone*
sordes, -is, f. *dirt, mourning*
soror, -ōris, f. *sister*
sortītio, -ōnis, f. *selection by lot*
spectāculum, -i, n. *sight*
spectātus, adj. *tested, esteemed*
specto, 1, *view, look for*
spēcula, -ae, f. *a bit of hope*
spēro, 1, *hope, expect*
spēs, spei, f. *hope, expectation*
splendor, -ōris, m. *excellence*
sponte suā, *of one's own free*
will, spontaneously
squālor, -ōris, m. *neglect,*
filthy clothes
statim, adv. *immediately*
statuo, 3, *determine*
status, -ūs, m. *state, condition,*
safety
sto, 1, steti, statum, *stand*
stomachor, 1, dep. *am angry,*
offended

strictim, adv. *superficially*

struo, 3, struxi, structum, *contrive*

studiōse, adv. *earnestly, carefully*

studium, -i, n. *pursuit, desire, application, goodwill*

stultitia, -ae, f. *stupidity, mad folly*

stultus, adj. *stupid, foolish*

subito, adv. *suddenly*

subitus, adj. *sudden*

sublātus, from tollo

sublevo, 1, *assist, acquit*

subsellium, -i, n. *bench, seat*

subvenio (venio), *help, preserve*

suffrāgium, -i, n. *vote*

summa, -ae, f. *total, amount*

summātim, adv. *shortly*

summus, adj. *highest, utmost, complete*

sūmo, 3, sumpsi, sumptum, *take, obtain*

sumptuōsus, adj. *extravagant*

sumptus, -ūs, m. *expense, cost*

superior, adj. *higher, former*

superstitio, -ōnis, f. *superstition, black magic*

superus, adj. *upper, above*

supplex, supplicis, adj. *suppliant*

supplicium, -i, n. *punishment, death*

supprimo (premo), *restrain, withhold*

suscipio (capio), *undertake, begin, acknowledge a child (§ 32)*

suspicio, -ōnis, f. *suspicion*

suspiciōsus, adj. *suspicious, suspected*

suspicor, 1, dep. *suspect*

sustuli, see tollo

T., abbrev. for Titus

tabella, -ae, f. *tablet, document*

taberna, -ae, f. *shop*

tabula, -ae, f. *waxed writing-tablet, account-book, record*

tacitus, adj. *silent*

tam, adv. *so*

tamdiū, adv. *for so long*

tamen, adv. *however, still, but*

tametsi, conj. *though*

tandem, adv. *at last*; in questions, *pray, I ask*

tanquam (tamquam), conj. *like, so to speak*

tantum, adv. *only*

tantus, adj. *so great*; hīc tantus, *this great*

Tarentum, -i, n. *Tarentum*

Teānum, -i, n. *Teanum*

tectum, -i, n. *roof, house*

tempus, -oris, n. *time, occasion, season*

teneo, 2, tenui, tentum, *hold, keep*

tento, 1, *try, test*

tenuis, adj. *slight*

terreo, 2, *terrify*

testāmentum, -i, n. *will*

testimōnium, -i, n. *evidence*

testis, -is, c. *witness, evidence*

testor, 1, dep. *declare, call to witness, invoke*

timeo, 2, *fear*

timor, -ōris, m. *fear*

tollo, 3, sustuli, sublātum, *remove, destroy*

tormentum, -i, n. *instrument of torture, torment*

tortor, -ōris, m. *torturer*

tortuōsus, adj. *twisted*

tot, indecl. adj. *so many*

tōtus, adj. *whole, entire*
tracto, 1, *investigate*
transcrībo (scrībo), 3, *copy*
transeo (eo), *pass over*
transfero (fero), *transfer*
transigo (ago), *transact, do a deal*
trēs, pl. adj. *three*
tribūniclus, adj. *of a tribune*
tribūnus, -i, m. *tribune, magistrate*
triennium, -i, n. *space of three years*
tristis, adj. *mournful*
triumpho, 1, *go in triumph*
triumvir, -i, m. *police-magistrate*
tum, conj. *at that time, then*
turba, -ae, f. *crowd*
turpis, adj. *base, disgraceful*
turpitūdo, -inis, f. *baseness*
tūtor, -ōris, m. *guardian, trustee*

ubi, conj. *where, when*
ullus, adj. *any, any other*
umquam, adv. *ever*
ūnā, adv. *together with*
unde, adv. *whence*
undecimus, adj. *eleventh*
undique, adv. *from everywhere*
ūnIversus, adj. *unanimous, one and all*
ūnus, adj. *one, only, alone, same;* ūnō tempore, *simultaneously*
ūnusquisque, pron. *each single one*
usque (ad), adv. *up to, as far as*
ut, conj. *in order that, so that, as, when, how* (§ 23)
uterque, utriusque, pron. *each of two, both*

ūtilis, adj. *useful*
ūtor, 3, ūsus, dep *use, know, am intimate with*
utrum...an, conj. *whether... or*
uxor, -ōris, f. *wife*

vagus, adj. *wandering*
valeo, 2, *am well; signify,* § 25
valētūdo, -inis, f. *health*
varius, adj. *changeful*
vehementer, adv. *severely, deeply, violently*
vēna, -ae, f. *vein*
venēficium, -i, n. *poisoning*
venēnum, -i, n. *poison*
vēneo (eo), *am for sale*
venio, 4, vēni, ventum, *come*
verbum, -i, n. *word*
vereor, 2, dep. *fear, revere*
vēritas, -ātis, f. *truth*
verso, 1, *turn, discuss*
versor, 1, dep. *am engaged in, concerned, involved*
vērum, adv. *but, certainly*
vērus, adj. *true, genuine*
vester, adj. *your, of yours*
vestIgium, -i, n. *footprint, track, clue, vestige*
vestIgo, 1, *track, find*
vestrum, genit. pl. of tu
vetus, veteris, adj. *old, old-fashioned*
vlātor, -ōris, m. *usher, apparitor*
vicinitas, -ātis, f. *neighbourhood, neighbours*
vicinus, -i, m. *neighbour*
victōria, -ae, f. *victory*
victrix, fem. adj. *victorious* (over)
video, 2, vīdi, vīsum, *see*
videor, 2, vīsus, dep. *seem*

vinco, 3, vīci, victum, *overcome*
vinoulum, -i, n. *chain, prison*
violo, 1, *defile*
vir, viri, m. *man, husband*
vires, vīrium, pl. f. *strength*
virtūs, -ūtis, f. *manliness, excellence, courage*
vīs, vim, vi, f. *force, punishment*
vīta, -ae, f. *life, lifetime*
vitium, -i, n. *vice, crime*
vitricus, -i, m. *stepfather*
vīvo, 3, vixi, victum, *am alive, live*

vīvus, adj. *alive, living*
vix, adv. *scarcely*
vōcīferātio, -ōnis, f. *cry, utterance*
volo, velle, volui, *am willing, wish, grant*
voluntas, -ātis, f. *intention, inclination*
vōtum, -i, n. *vow, offering*
vox, vōcis, f. *word, voice, cry*
vulnus, -eris, n. *wound, shock*
vultus, -ūs, m. *face, looks*